The Riehl Interaction Model in Action

BETTY KERSHAW

Principal
Stockport, Tameside and Glossop College of Nursing

and

BOB PRICE

BA, MSc, SRN, Cert.Ed. (Education)

Vice Principal
Dept of Education, The Royal Marsden Hospital
London

Series Editor
BOB PRICE

MACMILLAN

First published 1993 by
THE MACMILLAN PRESS LTD
Houndmills, Basingstoke, Hampshire RG21 2XS
and London
Companies and representatives
throughout the world

ISBN 0–333–57277–7

A catalogue record for this book is available from the British Library

Typeset by TecSet Ltd, Wallington, Surrey.

Printed in Hong Kong

CONTENTS

When we set out to create this series, it was an explicit goal that we would seek to explain, and help interpret, the theorist's nursing care model in a wide contextual arena and with a view to the most modern nursing circumstances prevailing. The tradition continues now, in this the Riehl Interaction Model volume of the series. Where it differs perhaps from its sister volumes is that the authors address a model which has received little exposure outside the United States of America. Moreover, unlike some of the macro-level models of the early 1960s and 1970s, it has not been obviously developed to anything like the same degree as, say, the work of Dorthea Orem or Sister Callista Roy. Betty Kershaw spells this out in Sections 1 and 3 of the present text. There are developmental gaps within the model and perhaps this has limited its application to settings in Britain and elsewhere. This has posed a new challenge to the series, and we as authors make no apology for playing our part in developing the Riehl model literature. We have been mindful to try to interpret our brief faithfully, to reflect the original concerns of Riehl-Sisca, but we own too, those enhancements of original principles, that we feel are a feature of these pages.

The goal is, we believe, very worthwhile. Riehl's work, based upon a substantial literature within sociology (the micro-level sociology of the symbolic interactionist school) has much to offer. We do live within a professional world where we are required to be much more conscious of all our nursing roles. We have to reflect not only on the care we deliver, but the manner of its delivery too. It can be cogently argued that both are integral, and the symbolic interaction of nurse–patient relationships is as much a part of care as any dressing or pain relief posture change. Because Riehl's model places great emphasis upon chosen, reciprocal roles, being reflexive as well as reflective, social as well as physical in our care – there is much to be gleaned here.

As you read through these sections (a review of the model, care study applications and critique) you may come to agree with Betty Kershaw, that the model is most suited to the experienced, primary care practitioner. Certainly, we cannot be naive, nurse–patient interaction may operate at a very sophisticated level. You may agree too that practice has to be bound by a professional confidentiality, a fellow traveller philosophy – that demands a great deal of the nurse. Even if this seems likely though, we both hope that you will not be daunted, but will actively explore the model in your clinical setting. We know that the assessment tool (FANCAP) is accessible to the neophyte nurse. We believe too that you will be familiar with the multiple roles of nursing – so the model need not be difficult for the student who is setting out on this particular journey.

The care studies offered here illustrate our point. A wide array of nurses employ the model, all with a basic level of success. There are different interpretations of what a care plan will look like. There are varying degrees of confidence shown concerning the development of interactive roles. Nevertheless, it's true too that all of the patients or clients benefit to a large extent, and the act of reflecting upon care roles nurtures the nurse as she develops her expertise. This text does not offer a dyed in the wool template for Riehl model care. This is as it should be, the studies building upon Riehl's concepts, and reflecting the special circumstances that confront each nurse. Care is always contextual, and models are the servant of skilful and sensitive practice. This is never more true than of the Riehl model, for if it has not been developed as much as most, neither has it been corrupted into a local, unbending dogma of how care must be delivered.

ACKNOWLEDGEMENTS

We should like to thank all our colleagues, family and friends who have shown patience, interest and encouragement during the preparation of this textbook.

In particular, we would like to acknowledge the assistance of Adrienne Hooper, our critical reader and enthusiastic supporter (Section 2). In reality only a few people may author a textbook, but many have helped to build it.

Bob Price
Betty Kershaw

Review of the Model

CHAPTER ONE

The model itself

Joan Riehl's work on her model appeared in Britain in 1980 (Riehl and Roy, 1980). Unlike most other American nurse theorists, her model appears to have had little application in the United Kingdom: indeed there is little published material in the USA or Canada either. One reason for this could be that the model is not one for the beginning practitioner. Another might be that those using it lack the confidence to go into print, while a third could lie within the conceptual framework on which the model is based. The theoretical framework of symbolic interaction is not easy to interpret into practice. As well as Riehl, Peplau (as discussed by Simpson, 1991) and King (1991) both use symbolic interactionism. Walsh (1991) correctly points out that most of the published material is in the field of psychiatric care. Riehl attempts to move the theory into a more general framework and this book moves with this attempt.

SYMBOLIC INTERACTION

In 1980 Riehl stated that the underlying perspective upon which her model is based is that of symbolic interactionism. Discussing the development of the conceptual framework for the model in her own works (Riehl and Roy, 1980; Riehl-Sisca, 1989) she gives a working definition as that of 'thinking behaviour' which 'controls the interaction that occurs between human beings who interpret or define each other's actions instead of merely reacting to them.' Responses to the communcations are based not only on the words themselves, but on the meaning and insight placed on them. The meaning and insight is based on role (patient, nurse, doctor), on place (hospital, home, school), on life experience and on the patient's state of mind. In order to use a model based on symbolic interaction the nurse needs to be 'a knowledgeable doer' (UKCC, 1986).

In 1986 Gochnauer and Miller critiqued Riehl's work, tracing the framework back into sociology and social psychology. They recognised that social interactionism acknowledges the inherent respect for human life that is the basis for the excellent nursing practice which demonstrates quality care.

Henderson (1966) writes of mind and body being inseparable, and of the need for the nurse to consider them as equally important. She writes of the nurse 'interpreting' for the patient (and family and friends) bringing into words what he or she cannot say for themselves. This Henderson defines as empathy and says that it 'requires a listening ear, constant observation and interpretation of non-verbal behaviour.' This level of communication requires the nurse to give of herself, sharing something of herself, her personality, her psychological expertise and her knowledge in order to develop the therapeutic partnership which is esssential to the practice of symbolic interaction as a nursing skill. Caring is based on the usual individual assessment, but the quality and the level of communication must involve high-level verbal and non-verbal interaction and well-developed interpretative skills.

Riehl's model is therefore developed from the most basic, and at the same time, most advanced, of nursing skills. The ideal concept of nurse:patient interaction becomes more complex as intelligence and knowledge are recognised and accepted within a person-to-person relationship. Riehl sees interaction as the unique way in which people relate one to another and her emphasis on the therapeutic use of interaction differentiates her model from the many others that merely use communication as a means of information gaining and transmitting.

The nurse planning to use Riehl's model of care must become skilled in interpreting her own and other's interactions. She must be able to empathise with those for whom she cares and must have a high level of interpretative ability relevant to the understanding of non-verbal communication. She needs a sound knowledge base for practice, and the ability to pre-empt requests for help and to assist patients and relatives in explaining and making clear what is hidden. She must be a pro-active communicator, able to use communication at its many levels and to use it therapeutically in such a way that the relationship is progressed. The nurse must be able to move from being a merely responsive communicator to one who can seek information and use it within the structured and caring relationship which is the lynchpin of successful nursing intervention.

Like all nursing models and their application to practice, the nurse will be comfortable using Riehl's model when she herself has chosen it (Wright, 1990a) and if the philosophical framework inherent in the model is congruent with how she wishes to give care. Riehl's model is not the model for the beginner to use alone. It can only be successfully applied by the competent nurse who is comfortable with herself and has a sound theoretical and practical base from which to develop interactive care. The exposure of self this model demands brings risks to both nurse and patient. It is possible that the recognition of risk has inhibited its use.

FURTHER EXPLORATION OF THE THEORETICAL FRAMEWORK

Riehl-Sisca (1989) recognised several key assumptions which underline the theoretical framework.

Assumption 1

Man lives in a symbolic community as well as in a physical environment. He can be 'stimulated' to act by symbols as well as by physical stimuli. At a basic stage, someone who has suffered pain at the dentist will associate a dental surgery with pain and will experience pain, even if there is no invasive treatment, merely a dental examination. More complicated is the culture and ethnicity that surrounds care. Certain cultures and ethnic groups have specific assumptions about childbirth, operative intervention, mental illness, death. These may be coloured by the environment and the new culture they have moved into, but will not be over-ridden. The nurse needs to understand and empathise with these cultural and ethnic expectations, and to take account of them in planning and giving care.

The value of community studies as part of nursing education has relevance to this assumption, enabling students to begin to develop that understanding of society which controls the behaviour of ourselves and those for whom we care.

Assumption 2

Through symbols, man has the capacity to stimulate others in ways other than those which are expected. This counsels us, perhaps even warns us, that we must be sure we are giving and receiving the message correctly. We must analyse communication to ensure the content is transmitted accurately and to do this we must develop analytic skills, based on sound and sincere interpretative listening. Only when we have, can our communication be the basis for care planning and intervention.

Self

Having internalised the nature of interactive communication the nurse who intends to use Riehl's model must then move to the understanding of 'self'. A person's self-concept is determined by his or her interaction with others. As outside stimuli affect his perception of self, this changes. Thus positive, supportive communication can enhance self-image or self-concept, while that which is critical can damage it. The nature of the human person is such that damage to the self-image lasts much longer than enhancement. For the nurse to be able to encourage interactive communication, she must have a 'good' self-concept, confident in her knowledge base or professional skill. She will also realise that those who are ill may have a lowered self-esteem, as may the relatives or friends who may also suffer feelings of guilt. The elderly patient who suffers the embarrassment of incontinence, the young mother who 'can't cope', the unemployed father, the hit-and-run driver – all suffer from the loss of self-value that affects their self-concept and self-esteem.

The empathy discussed earlier then becomes of paramount importance, and the nurse who is confident and comfortable with herself will be able to relax enough to be empathic. Thus the nurse not only needs to understand and appreciate her own self, but she also needs to understand and interpret that of her patient and his family.

Role

The theoretical framework for self-concept impinges closely on that of 'role', in as much as one's self-esteem is often based on role and role perception. A business man, on becoming ill, may no longer feel in control of his business. His self-esteem suffers, because he can no longer function in his role. A hospitalised mother will have her own role as a parent threatened when someone else has to care for a child. Similarly, the nurse may experience loss of role confidence if she is moved to working in an environment different from her own and where her skills and competence are questioned. She will also lose role confidence if required to work in an unfamiliar way, or with a framework for care which lacks congruence with her own (Wright, 1990a).

Riehl recognises that role confidence depends on environment and self-perception. She acknowledges that nurses experience conflict in their role as nurses when they are required to carry out actions which distress them, even if the distress is not related to their nursing role. A nurse may find it very difficult to carry out a task, for example an injection to a child who is frightened, if it causes stress to another of her roles – in this case, that of the mother.

Role conflict

What Riehl doesn't ever really recognise is the role-conflict inherent in nursing. Role conflict happens when a person's roles clash. In nursing today (1993) many nurses are faced with decision-making about care based on finance. Their budgetary management role conflicts with their caring function. Nurses may find themselves guided into decision-making, or even controlling discussions, which are based on the realistic help they can give rather than what is best. They learn to work within the parameters of what is possible and achievable, thus maintaining their role status (as a competent, successful practitioner) and their own self-esteem.

Role relationship

The Riehl Interaction model is dependent on the relationships built up between nurse and patient, and these are explored later within the case study examples. Initially they are two people meeting as independent persons, who have to move into a positive and support-ive relationship. Although at no time does Riehl mention it, this development of role support one-to-another appears to require a primary nursing approach (Wright, 1990b), or at the very least the 'named nurse' of the Patient's Charter (HMSO, 1991). It is difficult to see how the model could be used without this mutual sharing. This will be explored later, and illustrated within the case studies. She describes how the nurse moves through roles during the nurse–patient relationship, perhaps beginning with the role of enquirer – she who asks the questions, moving on to problem-solver – she who uses the answers to produce the care plan. The nurse then becomes the care-giver, the teacher of self-care, perhaps the change agent who helps temporary or permanent adaptation, and finally the professional friend (Figure 1.1).

Figure 1.1   *Examples of nurse–patient–family reciprocal relationships (adapted from Riehl-Sisca, 1989)*

Patient/significant other roles	Possible nurse roles
Problem aware individual/family	Problem solver
Care recipient	Care provider
Learner	Teacher
Copee	Coper (facilitator)
Decision taker	Decision facilitator
Change agent novice	Change agent
Active problem solver	Role model

There are similarities between Riehl's model and the philosophical framework for care explored by Alistair Campbell (1984). Campbell defines professional care as 'moderated love, which combines necessary detachment with a concern for individual values and socio-political change'. He refers to care-giving as 'skilled companionship', likening it to a journey where the care-giver (in this case the nurse but the framework can equally be applied to therapists, doctors, chaplains) assists the patient and family through the nursing trajectory knowing that as health returns, or a peaceful death ensues, the journey will end. Within the journey, the nurse and patient will play many roles, but the roles will be constantly changing and adapting, thereby minimising the pain that comes within a relationship that becomes too role-dependent.

PRIMARY ROLE

Perhaps then, for all it's sociological and psychological framework Riehl's model is not that complicated to use. The nurse is a change-agent, basing her changing care on sound assessment, nursing skill and patient adaption. Her role encourages self-care and leads the patient through competent care-planning, giving and reviewing, into role security and, once more, a positive self-image.

CHAPTER TWO

The process of nursing

Riehl acknowledges that the interpretation of theory into practice is through a structured approach to care planning, delivery and review. British nurses best recognise this as the nursing process. Riehl-Sisca (1989) suggests the use of a problem-solving approach as outlined by Stevens (1984): 'The process is initiated when a problem is encountered. Secondly, there is as much discussion as necessary among the patient, family and nurse to identify the problem and possible solutions. Finally, and most importantly, the correct diagnosis of the problem must be determined'.

The nurse using Riehl's model will obviously bring her self-perception, her understanding of the patient's perception of self (the role) and interpret this into the care planning by skill in interactive and reactive communication. To aid the problem-solving process, Riehl recommends the use of FANCAP as outlined by Abbey (1980). Abbey describes FANCAP 'as a framework for concepts, the purpose of which is to discover patient-care problems and propose solutions for them' . . . 'FANCAP organises impressions, solutions and related nursing intervention into a nursing care plan'.

The letters of FANCAP (a mnemonic) serve as the 'pegs' to hang ideas on, and stand for Fluids, Aeration, Nutrition, Communication, Activity and Pain. The headings (or pegs) in themselves inspire the knowledgeable nurse to ask the correct questions to begin the problem-solving approach.

Aeration not only applies to oxygen flow and exchange but leads into the ventilation of feelings (psychological) and into the realms of poor housing, undernourishment, allergies (with their many social connotations) because of the implications of these situations on respiratory health. Like the model itself, FANCAP needs skill and knowledge to use. The case study examples demonstrate its application to practice most competently. Pearson (1983) describes its use in the UK as does Walsh (1991). Sadly though, like the model, its use is little documented.

Arumugam (1985) appears to have published the first, and possibly the only, example of Riehl's model applied to care in the UK. He uses the model successfully within a psychiatric setting and continues to develop his interest, publishing again in 1989. Both works used Abbey's interpretation of FANCAP, as does the essay by Aggleton and Chalmers in the same 1989 publication.

All illustrate clearly how FANCAP can be used to demonstrate and interpret the theoretical framework into practice. Using the mnemonic, and applying Abbey's 'peg-hanging' as she suggests:

Fluids – liquids capable of flowing
Aeration – exposing, breathing, ventilation
Nutrition – nourishing, caring, loving, friendship, support
Communication – interacting
Activity – work, play, learning, socialising
Pain – physical, psychological, social, loss

the nurse can cover all the points of any nursing assessment. The six concepts are multi-disciplinary in nature, moving through all the systems of the body and into the psychological aspects of society. Nothing is forgotten: everything of relevance is addressed and noted.

CORE ELEMENTS

To move through the application of the model, the nurse needs to understand one more aspect of underlying theory, besides that of the model itself, and the means of interpreting it into action – in this case FANCAP.

All models and theories recognise four core elements. Sometimes the names change, but the same key concepts are clearly defined. The interpretation the theorist lays on these key elements defines further the application to practice and, alongside the assumptions, these elements need to be considered as the framework for care develops.

Riehl-Sisca (1989) defines these key concepts as: *person* (other theorists refer to this as *man* – a human being, a genetically and socially emergent self). This links back into the care assumptions of role and self-image/concept, recognising the importance that both the individual's family and inheritance have had on shaping his or her perceptions, and how these perceptions are linked with the society, culture, religion and ethnic group within which the patient lives. The nurse, using Riehl's model, will recognise how all these factors affect the way the individual communicates and reacts to situations such as ill-health, hospitalisation or stress. For example, a child on being admitted to hospital will be separated from family, friends and a familiar environment. The nurse will familiarise herself as soon as possible with such issues as previous admissions, whether or not the child was prepared for admission, what he or she understands about it, what frightens him or her, what comforts him or her, and (most importantly) whether or not his or her parents are able to stay or visit frequently. She will seek to understand the person – whether as child, son or daughter – and the child's self-concept – how comfortable he or she feels with the admission. Based on this knowledge she will use her communication skills, and the FANCAP tool, to begin her nursing assessment.

ENVIRONMENT

Environment is defined be Riehl as the conditions which influence the emergent self. The self then continually and constantly interacts with the external and internal conditions which mould and shape the society and culture within which the man moves. To revert back to the example of the child given earlier – by thoroughly analysing previous case records, by utilising information from admissions data, by using knowledge from her own experience and understanding of the child's community, the nurse can 'set the scene' to provide, as far as is possible, an environment that encourages the development of the therapeutic relationship. The child, like any other patient, will be more secure re-admitted to a familiar ward. Younger children need playthings, school facilities and resident parents. Older children or teenagers like Graydon (Chapter 4) may wish to be nursed with adults or in a sideward which ensures their privacy. Facilities for family (and increasingly friends) are important in creating an environment, as are the means of continuing to enjoy music, television and videos appropriate to their age.

NURSING

Nursing is defined by Riehl as 'therapeutic action that guides the nurse–patient relationship', enabling the patient to achieve the best possible quality of life and reach his potential. The child in hospital will be encouraged to participate in play with friends, to continue schooling, to enjoy visits from family and friends, and to listen to the music he plays at home. Care will be taken to ensure that the customs of home can be practised, and that he remains in touch with the peer-group activities of his age. Nursing goes far beyond mere physical acts of caring, the nurse becoming the travelling companion of Campbell, being playmate, teacher, parent, all in turn, changing role as the child changes his.

HEALTH

Health (sometimes called Wellness) is defined by Riehl as 'an individual's perception', monitored by self and peers, which is arrived at in communication with others and changes through time depending on the physiological, social and psychological framework and the stresses which disturb the individual's equilibrium. Thus a person with diabetes may define himself as 'well' because the disease is controlled and he lives a normal satisfactory life, while his mother (who sees the disease from the perspective of 'incurable' and 'constant diet and drugs') will describe him as ill. The physically or mentally handicapped person may consider themselves, and be considered by peers, to be healthy only to be reminded of their condition when access to public transport or buildings proves impossible. The social and environmental effects on health are clearly demonstrated in that example while psychological attitudes so easily cause the stigma of 'ill-health' when people speak to the person walking with the blind man and not the man himself. The excellent BBC Radio 4 series *Does he take sugar?* illustrates many more examples. The nurse working with Riehl's model will ensure that such attitudes (in herself and others) are not allowed to become entrenched.

A FRAMEWORK FOR PRACTICE

We have already considered how Riehl's model develops into a basis for practice and how she recommends its application, using FAN-CAP, into the problem-solving assessment and through the other stages of the nursing process. The nurse supports the patient through the care-giving stage, developing changes in role as the patient moves from sickness to health. The value the model places on therapeutic communication is acknowledged and the need for the nurse to be clinically competent is inherent in the interpretation of theory to practice.

Riehl's 1980 work was very much a theory: her 1989 publication moved it into practice. Bridge and Macleod-Clark (1981) published one of the earliest British texts expanding the value of therapeutic communication, and explored the need for nurses to listen, to develop counselling skills, to search for the less obvious answers and to understand the non-verbal messages. Increasingly, British nurses have based their care-planning on such interactions.

Riehl is very much a model for the 1990s, encouraging reflective practice (Benner, 1984) and the need for nursing care to be based on a soundly researched tool. In Riehl's case, there is little evidence of a clinical research base in the few publications relating to either her own work or to FANCAP. Hopefully this text will begin to redress this situation. The model needs to be viewed within the context of 1992.

THE PATIENT'S CHARTER (1991)

In November 1991, Her Majesty's Government published the Patient's Charter (HMSO, 1991). In it they defined their commitment to the National Health Service (NHS) and set out their goals for the next few years. Regardless of the rise in private health insurance (WPA Annual Report, 1990) many people still have expectations of the NHS, and their use of it, which run counter to modern nursing approaches such as self-care, adaption and care in the community.

Most people still expect to use the NHS only when they are ill, therefore any individual utilising health-care services must mean they are 'ill' (or at the very least 'unwell'). Nurses therefore care for the sick, and are thus associated with sickness. Furthermore, people who have health problems, who see themselves as ill because nurses are working with them or caring for them, still expect to be cared for in institutions. The changing role of the nurse as health provider, health educator, partner in care and rehabilitation is still not fully recognised. This leads to inevitable role conflict between nurse and patient and carer and cared-for. Concepts and self-concepts differ too. The need for the general public to recognise this changing role is necessary for the implementation of the quality health objectives in the Patient's Charter.

Nurses have recognised their changing role for many years. The Patient's Charter talks of 'a named nurse or midwife', while Wright

(1990b) and Ersser (1991) define Primary Nursing, whereby one nurse has the key responsibility for the patient's care planning and interpretation. This approach must be essential when using Riehl's model since the confidential relationship and therapeutic communication demands cannot work if confidential discussions are open to anyone other than on a 'need-to-know' basis.

The concept of primary nursing and named nurses may indeed differ in practice. But the key responsibility, the prime carer, is acknowledged in both. One hopes the setting-up of clinical directorates will encourage responsibility for patients across the wider area of care with one nurse moving with her patient through clinics as well as ward units. The community nursing centres already practice such an approach to care. *My Patient* (Wright, 1990b) is not an unusual concept for the elderly person who has the same district nurse three days each week.

As the profession moves to more wider implementation of this aspect of the Patient's Charter (and indeed moves to meet the challenge of the other key objectives), nurses need to work within a framework that recognises their skills, knowledge and professional competence. Riehl's model offers this.

Care Study Applications

The care studies: introductory notes

Six very different care studies are laid out here to help you to interpret Riehl's model and examine its usefulness in contrasting clinical care settings. We won't pretend that the nurses have taken a uniform approach, or that all care has been one hundred per cent successful. Instead, we argue that authentic care (warts and all) is creative, not invariably successful, but worthwhile despite this, as long as we learn important lessons from it. These then are not cardboard cut out patients or situations, but representations of nursing reality. We trust that they will ring familiar bells with you as you read through them and consider the associated self-check questions and review exercises.

In the first (James Drew) you are introduced to the FANCAP assessment tool and helped to consider its usefulness in the burns unit setting. It can be fairly argued that the nurses looking after James have not worked out all their care roles at the most conscious level. Even so, the role relationships with patient and relatives are exposed for your further exploration.

Turning to Graydon Powell (and the challenge of Hodgkin's disease), this theme of interaction between nurse, patient and relatives is further developed. These nurses (and in particular his primary nurse) are very *au fait* with the way in which role adoption and change may have a profound effect upon care. The nurses use the role that they are playing to negotiate a package of support that will encourage Graydon to maintain control and a sense of dignity. Just as sophisticated is the care delivered to Irene Watkins in care study three. While Irene is not in need of direct physical intervention, and maintains a lot of independence within the community – this does not mean that the nurse cannot develop therapeutic interaction with Irene herself and those people that she encounters.

Relatively few models have been examined in the community context, but Irene Watkins' situation forms a useful testing ground for the Riehl interaction model.

Interaction of course is not limited to nurses, the patient and their significant others. Nurses work in a multidisciplinary setting and it may be the case that negotiated relationships with colleagues will affect (for good or ill) the well-being of the patient. This area of concern is explored in Chapter 6. It is an account of care that should have progressed quite smoothly, but which did not, in part because of communication difficulties. The Riehl model helps Helen Gower to take stock of her professional actions, and this is an important aspect of practice. Too often, evaluation as a stage of care has been neglected or confined to whether the patient recovered and was satisfied.

In the penultimate care study, we turn to a mental health/ community setting, and the often unrecognised work of the Community Psychiatric Nurse (CPN). Evette Lloyd's bulimia problem is not a simple one, nor is her personal circumstance one that is easily assessed or adjusted, in answer to this challenge. This care study emphasises how a model can be part of a longer term support, sharing in the unfinished symphony that characterises much of nursing care. There is an argument that this model has helped the CPN to structure her care more efficiently – to conceptualise a significant, yet often hidden problem. You of course will judge whether it helped you to understand the problems, and whether it enhanced Evette's care!

Last, but certainly not least, Carla Moore. Carla you will discover is not a patient, but a Staff Nurse on a High Dependency Care Unit. In a very real sense, though, she is a client of John Evans (the ward tutor and mentor) who visualises her support as part of a Riehl inspired package to reduce the risk of burnout on the ward. Caring extends to colleagues as well as to patients, and in this last study, we invite you to explore whether a nursing model might not help us to deal with these needs just as ably as with patient care ones.

Six studies then, all very different. The stories have been based upon real experiences, by real nurses, with all names adjusted to preserve anonymity. We hope that the untidiness of real care situations, the swings and roundabouts of care effort, will help you to look critically at Riehl's model and some of its possible applications and developments.

CHAPTER THREE

James Drew: the burn victim

INTRODUCTION

Three days ago James Drew was busy burning the brush wood that resulted from his work as a landscape gardener. James was a new apprentice to this work and at the age of nineteen sometimes tended to cut corners. The addition of some kerosene, to get the bonfire burning properly, proved a major mistake. James suffered burns to both his arms, the front of his chest and the right side of his face. Luckily the garden owner was present and immediately summoned an ambulance. James was admitted to the hospital burns unit via casualty. James was assessed to have suffered 30 per cent burns of which 15 per cent (his arms) were described as partial thickness.

The burns unit staff initiated emergency care, including a full assessment of James' breathing, his airway and the degree of hypovolaemic shock. Controlled oxygen therapy was commenced, and an intravenous cannula introduced into his right leg. Using the Muir and Barclay scale (Muir et al., 1987), an intravenous fluid regime of dextran was started, to continue throughout the shock period (72 hours). In addition, intravenous morphine was administered to relieve James' considerable pain.

James was cared for in the protective environment of the shock room. He received wound toilet, the burns of his hands being covered with silver sulphadiazine cream and then in plastic bag dressings. His arms and chest also received a coating of silver sulphadiazine before being dressed in an occlusive dressing. As each procedure was prepared, the nurse explained what would happen, reassuring him that this would assist his recovery and limit the risks of infection. It was explained to him that the catheterisation of his urinary bladder would enable the nurse to assess his fluid balance accurately over the coming days. The nasogastric tube introduced would enable the nurse to aspirate stomach juices and decompress the stomach which might otherwise prove uncomfortable. James' parents arrived two hours after his admission and they too received a briefing about his care.

Today, James moves out of the shock room and into his own room within the burns unit. The care plan to date has featured support of his vital functions, rather less has been done towards meeting his psychological and social needs. As James moves toward the rehabilitation phase of his care, the nurse prepares a thorough assessment of his condition, utilising the Riehl interaction model.

FANCAP ASSESSMENT

Now that James was beginning to express his fears and questions about his injuries and the future – it was germane to establish his perspective on what was happening to him. The patient who suffers a major burn may not begin to develop a considered position on his situation until after the initial shock period (Avni, 1980; Patterson, 1987). During that time he has experienced sensory deprivation and sensory overload as a result of the protective environment of the shock room and the intensive care necessary there. Now that vital functions are rather more stable, James begins to experience a 'flood response' (Price, 1990), with the full enormity of his problems becoming apparent to him.

Fluids

Physiologically, James' fluid balance is much improved. His intravenous infusion is still *in situ*, but he has now moved into the diuretic phase and is producing appreciable quantities of urine. James has started to take sips of water, something that he demands on an hourly basis because his mouth feels dry and uncomfortable. It is anticipated that oral fluid intake will continue to increase and that this in turn will enable the staff to remove both the nasogastric tube and the intravenous infusion.

Through discussion during an evening shift, it is clear that James is starting to become more active in his situation. In the shock room he was completely passive, almost a receptacle for the care delivered. Now he has started to recall how he felt about this period, saying that he was angry at the intrusions into his privacy. James is starting to negotiate his care, and given his strong willed nature (reported by his parents), this seems likely to increase.

Aeration

James continues to show marked dyspnoea and difficulty in expectorating sputum. He has developed a productive cough and a sputum specimen has been sent to the laboratory for micro culture and sensitivity. His dyspnoea seems related to his chest dressings, pain on breathing deeply and the residual effects of inhaled smoke. A possible chest infection may also be exacerbating the situation. Baseline observations reveal a respiratory rate of 25 respirations a minute, each shallow and noisy. James has a pyrexia of 37.4°C, which may also be indicative of a chest infection.

James is now beginning to express his feelings about his early treatment and to complain volubly about his daily wound toilet. He has sworn at several nurses either for not waiting for his pre-dressing analgesia to work, or because his dressing change is seen as degrading. He expresses disgust at the fluid which collects around his burned fingers, and at the smell he associates with sweat and the dressings soaked in burn exudate. James has not expressed a view on his accident or his parents' upset. His employer has visited but no reports of James' feelings about the incident were forthcoming.

Nutrition

The burn, and enforced cessation of food intake during the shock period, have meant that James has become malnourished. Prior to the accident he was considered 'a little plump' by his mother – now he looks quite thin. As the burn oedema subsides and James starts to complain of a 'sore bottom' it becomes urgently clear that he will need protein, carbohydrate and trace element replacements. Provided that his oral fluids are well tolerated he will start a light high protein diet tomorrow.

James receives daily visits from both his parents, and seems well supported with news from home and practical items such as a personal stereo. James however dislikes his mother's visits, stating that he feels 'mollycoddled'. He seems to prefer the more business-like approach of his father.

Communication

As the facial odema has receded it is apparent that James will require early skin grafting to his right eyelid. James reports that he can see out of this eye and that he is more concerned with his sense of touch. He feels that his hands 'are seizing up', and this worries him because he has always worked with his hands. He has been given two very factual, even blunt, interviews by the consultant plastic surgeon. Despite being told about skin grafting for eyelid and hands, and a prolonged period of physiotherapy and pressure dressings, James states that the doctor probably overestimates the time and effort necessary to achieve an acceptable recovery.

The move out of the shock room is seen by James as a positive step. He does not however like the idea of the next step, into communal areas of the 'plastic ward'. Fears about the reactions of other patients toward his scarring and his inability to account for his new body image have made him reticent about mobilising very far.

Activity

James is visited daily by the physiotherapist, who teaches him deep breathing and helps him to expectorate sputum from his lungs. Physiotherapy to his burnt hands is proving a difficult process, James has limited flexion and extension in his fingers. The nurses repeat these exercises with James and assist him to walk around his room. This James does grudgingly, claiming that the nurses are hard taskmasters. In the light of James' limited exercise tolerance, the nurse assesses his circulation – there is no sign of a deep vein thrombosis or other vasculature complications.

Up until this point, James has not invested into education about his physiotherapy or the future value of skin grafting and pressure dressings. It is unclear whether this is because James is still dealing with grief at the loss of body image (Kubler Ross, 1970; Parkes, 1975) or because he is having difficulty understanding the length and process necessary for rehabilitation. He has undergone a rapid transition of role from young and fit employee to acutely ill patient – from a highly mobile adult male to a largely immobile man.

Pain

During the shock period James received regular doses of morphine. Since leaving the shock room this has been changed to pethidine. He

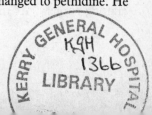

receives a dose of this drug prior to major wound toilet and dressing changes. In order to assess the effectiveness of the analgesia, James has been given his own pain chart, on which he plots the level and location of pain (Hunt *et al.*, 1977; Raiman, 1986). It is clear that James has a peak of pain during the first two hours' post dressings and early in the morning, after he has been lying still for a longer period of time. High levels of pain in the morning seem to correlate with a limited quantity of sleep achieved during the preceding night.

NURSING DIAGNOSIS

From this assessment the nurse concluded that to date James had not come to terms with his sudden injury or the rehabilitation that would be necessary afterwards. He had previously committed himself to his new adult working role which involved considerable independence and a responsibility to get on with his work. Now his burns required a completely different role and one that initially forced him to accept care passively. Suffering hypovolaemic shock, nursed in a strange environment and naked save for covering sheet, James was unable to negotiate a satisfactory definition of the situation. His situation had been imposed upon him, both by the nature of his injury and by his limited physical capacity to actively debate or co-operate in care.

Quite unintentionally, the nurses and doctors had inflicted a degradation ceremony (Goffman, 1961) upon James. His personal clothing and possessions had been set to one side and he was positioned supine in an arena where all the other actors retained their symbols of authority (such as uniforms and stethoscopes). Given these events, and James' previous strong will and early work career, it was not surprising that he was displaying a degree of role inflexibility. He was struggling to deal with the role of dependent patient throughout the shock period and was now being increasingly invited to become decision-taker and change agent (Riehl-Sisca, 1989, p 389). James was also struggling with a perceived role inflexibility in his mother, who was seeming to want to intrude excessively.

Part of James' role inflexibility was concerned with his current difficulties in learning about his care and general rehabilitation. Anger, denial, his grief in general, and an unrealistic appraisal of his natural ability to recuperate, were all inhibiting the uptake of patient education offered by nurse, physiotherapist and surgeon alike. This would pose a considerable problem as he underwent future skin grafting surgery. At that time, the anaesthetic and post-operative care would demand that he adopt a more passive role once again. James was tending to view his rehabilitation as a linear and uncomplicated process. He had not understood that there would be 'ups and downs' ahead and that he would have to work co-operatively with his carers, viewing them as colleagues rather than as agents of potential humiliation.

In the light of these considerable role transition challenges, it would be necessary to devise a care plan which put his physical care in the context of how he perceived himself, and his contribution to rehabilitation. The nurse would have to adopt a teaching and counselling role in order to help James to negotiate actively his future care.

CARE PLAN FOR JAMES AND HIS PARENTS

(see Table 3.1)

Now that James had reached the diuretic stage of his recovery, it was important to ensure that he did not become further dehydrated. The increased loss of fluids, both through diuresis and insensible loss through the skin, could also result in electrolyte (sodium or potassium) disturbance and acid–base imbalance. Against this, injudicious increase in oral fluids, alongside a continuing intravenous fluid regime, could lead to fluid overload.

The nurse discussed James' dehydrated state with the surgeon, highlighting his reluctance to mobilise and the problems this was posing for skin care. She reported his respiratory difficulties and acknowledged that it would be difficult to monitor fluid balance by observations of respiratory function (risk of pulmonary oedema) because of James' already dubious pulmonary condition. Having listened to his abdomen with the stethoscope, she was able to report to the physician that clear bowel sounds were now present and that James was not experiencing nausea as a result of his current oral intake of water.

In the light of these facts and a further medical examination and blood tests for serum electrolytes, James' oral fluid allowance was increased to 60 ml hourly. The surgeon and nurse took time to explain the cautious steps they were taking, as they increased fluid intake and monitored James for unwanted side effects. Should James tolerate the increased fluid, and prove patient with this regime, his nasogastric tube might be removed the next day. James said that he found the slow progress frustrating but that he was willing to persevere in order to get rid of his 'nose tube'. At this stage it was

Table 3.1 *James Drew: care plan*

Nursing diagnosis	Goal	Nursing interventions
Fluid problems		
1a Inadequate oral fluid intake (reliance on IVI)	Patient will consume increasing quantities of oral fluid within parameters advised by doctor	1. Reassess patient's tolerance of oral fluids and bowel sounds. Liaise with doctor to increase fluid intake to 60 ml hourly 2. Explain to James the benefits of same (with reference to removal of nasogastric tube and IV infusion) 3. Discuss with James benefits of oral fluids with reference to wound healing 4. Monitor fluid intake/output. Chart same
1b Dry uncomfortable mouth/skin associated with hypovolaemia	Patient will accept assistance in completing oral/skin toilet using preferred requisites	1. Assess James' capacity to accept assistance with hygiene care 2. Agree protocol for same, choosing times and practices 3. Re-emphasise the transitory nature of such assistance; as his hands improve this role will revert to James
1c Patient sees care staff as invading his personal space and privacy	Patient will view nursing staff as therapeutic, care measures as constructive	1. Explore with James his perceptions of previous care instructions 2. Discuss the changing roles, relevant now that he can control more body functions 3. Agree etiquette for future care
Aeration problems		
2a Dyspnoea (linked to pain,	Patient will view dyspnoea as a challenge and partake	1. Administer prescribed controlled 02 therapy 2. Monitor respiratory function 4 hourly

Problem	Goal	Nursing intervention
chest burns and smoke inhalation)	in measures to alleviate problem	3. Position patient upright to facilitate breathing 4. Teach patient how to support wounds when expectorating 5. Teach patient deep breathing exercises
2b Patient swears at staff when he feels frustrated and angry about his care	Patient will express his feelings in a mutually agreed manner	1. Review with James the frustrations and discomfort associated with care measures 2. Explore with him the significance of the same (*vis-à-vis* previous problems) 3. Arrange daily speak-easy sessions as an outlet for his anger
2c Patient experiences disgust at sight of his hands	James will be able to express an appreciation of why his hands are as they are	1. Provide daily dressing changes (hands) 2. Teach James the function of silver sulphadiazine 3. Explain that physiotherapy will improve function/appearance of hands 4. Take sequence photographs to prove same
2d Patient feels embarrassed at body odour associated with dressings (altered body image)	James will plan with the nurse wound and dressing care designed to enhance body hygiene	1. Daily change of dressings, or more frequently if dressings become soaked through 2. Deodorants utilised on unaffected skin 3. Patient assisted with washing, nail and hair care 4. Recheck all dressings before visiting times

Nutrition problems

Problem	Goal	Nursing intervention
3a Patient in a catabolic state	Patient will re-establish an acceptable nutritional state through oral diet	1. Patient introduced to hospital dietician: nutrition programme planned 2. Assist patient to eat meals (for example, cut up food, check size and frequency of meals) 3. Monitor patient's weight gain and exercise tolerance

3b Patient at risk of pressure sore formation	Patient will take necessary measures (assisted) to limit risk of pressure sore formation	1. Assess pressure areas 2 hourly using locally preferred risk assessment scale 2. Assist patient to move his position 2 hourly 3. Instruct him in use of monkey pole with reference to same 4. Check air flow mattress functioning (hourly)
3c Patient perceives his mother's concern as overpowering	Patient will successfully renegotiate son and mother roles in the light of his age and rehabilitation needs	1. James is assisted to clarify his feelings about mother's care 2. Mother assisted to discriminate between care giver and parental role 3. James advised how to point out acceptable care assistance to his mother
Communication problems		
4a Patient has limited range of vision due to right eyelid damage	Patient will successfully prepare for necessary skin grafting	1. Advocate James' concerns about his hands to surgeon; request that he in turn explains rationale of skin grafting sequence 2. Introduce James to successful patients who have already undergone skin grafting
4b Patient has limited sense of touch in his hands	Patient will co-operate with physiotherapist and nurses to improve hand function	1. Process of wound changes and contraction explained to James 2. Negotiate with James a physiotherapy programme designed to protect and enhance hand function 3. Reassure James that improvement in sensation may occur over time, but that sustained physiotherapy efforts will be important
4c James has formed an unrealistic idea of	Patient will revise his estimate of recovery, taking	1. Prepare folio of records that help James to assess realistic pace of progress (including weekly photographs, daily

		(audiotape diary and review of care plan)
how long it will take to rehabilitate	into account his injuries, the role of therapists and his role as patient	2. Discuss with James the physiology of wound changes over months
		3. Reiterate importance of skin grafting
		4. Assist James to revalue smaller progress steps
		5. Ask his parents to reinforce and value the same
		6. Praise James on all efforts – physiotherapy, tolerance of dressings
4d Patient anxieties at further rehabilitation contact with other people	James will (with support) plan strategies to help him form a new definition of his situation	1. Review with James his previous body image and concept of personal worth
		2. Reinforce that personal worth can evolve from strength of character as well as body appearance
		3. Introduce Burns Association counsellor to James (someone who has previously dealt with this stage)
		4. Plan limited trips to communal areas, with nurse support and debrief afterwards
		5. Review personal photographs – value improvements in appearance
		6. Help James to rehearse personal verbal accounts of his appearance and injury as he prefers

Activity problems

5a Immobility associated with pain and limitations of IV infusion	Patient will mobilise using a previously agreed programme	1. Review James' pain chart and discuss with him the extent to which this limits movement
		2. Remove IV infusion as soon as physician will sanction movement
		3. Teach James a range of movement exercise sequence for when he is sitting still
		4. Adminster prescribed analgesic prior to major physiotherapy efforts

Problem	Goal	Nursing intervention
		5. Develop a gradually more demanding series of walks for James
		6. Recheck all dressings and attachments beforehand
		7. Monitor patient's degree of exhaustion
5b Patient fails to internalise patient education on future surgery and the value of pressure dressings	Patient will revalue the learning role inherent in patient status, using same to promote role change back to independence	1. Explore with James the foundation of his health beliefs. Have these been accurate during preceding care?
		2. Examine with him his impressions of the way advice/education was offered
		3. Agree preferred learning strategy
		4. Utilise same to adjust patient education

Pain

Problem	Goal	Nursing intervention
6a Pain inadequately controlled during and after dressings	Patient will review pain relief with nurse and agree new measures to attain comfort	1. Examine key elements of dressing which cause pain; note these down
		2. Review James' confidence in pre-dressing analgesia
		3. Discuss measures that James uses to cope with pain (such as tensing up muscles)
		4. Agree a package of patient, nurse and medication measures (the latter through consultation with doctor) to explore future pain control
6b Pain disrupting or exacerbating sleep pattern problems	James and nurse will review night care in order to limit sleep disturbance and reduce morning pain	1. Draw up outline diary of typical night's care and blocks of sleep for James
		2. Map any daytime sleep
		3. Adjust evening/night care regime by negotiation with James
		4. Administer prescribed medications and critically examine benefits/effects

still unclear whether he understood the benefit to his wounds of becoming rehydrated. James appeared to think through a very practical, concrete frame of mind. The removal of the nasogastric tube, and improved comfort in his mouth, would be tangible; wound changes associated with rehydration of the body might not!

It was clear that James was becoming increasingly fed up with feeling unclean and sweaty. He was more than willing to accept assistance with oral hygiene and the more general areas of skin care. At this point it seemed possible that he might even come to rely on the nurses' help, and prove in turn less willing to take control of washes once more himself. A second, male nurse, was able to reassure the team in this regard however. While this nurse would prepare flannel and towels for perineal hygiene, he insisted that James would wash (however clumsily), and he would dry. In this way perineal skin would remain properly clean, there would be limited physiotherapy for James' plastic bagged hands, and a start point for the return of self-care would be assured. All such washes were in addition to dressing changes in the burns unit bath.

Because James complained of oral discomfort, special attention was paid to this aspect of care. The nurse reassessed his dentition and the mucosa, looking for signs of trauma or infection. His mouth was obviously dehydrated but there was no sign of fungal or other forms of infection. She asked James what his preferences on oral care were. Using a mug of mouthwash he could be in control, the nurse merely holding the receiver for him. Manipulating a toothbrush at this stage would require more assistance. James explained that he was worried about how his front teeth looked to any visitors, so a 'toothbrush session' around midday and early evening were important. Early morning and late evening, mouth washes could then be used to complete the plan. Both agreed on this, the nurse promising to add vaseline to his lips on a day-to-day basis. The care plan was adjusted accordingly.

Having worked out an agreed protocol for additional washes, skin, nose and oral hygiene care, the nurse proposed a daily check on nail and hair condition. The high temperature of the burns unit would make James hair matted and unpleasant for him. That hair which could be washed on a regular basis (without interfering with the burn) should be. James had not thought about his hair but readily agreed that it would be useful to receive such care.

The new plan of hygiene care had been running 48 hours when the nurse took the opportunity to explore James' previous perceptions of nursing care. It was evening and despite feeling tired James was keen to remark on how the nurses now seemed to respect him more. He was satisfied that his current hygiene care was a shared effort that had been properly planned. The nurse asked James whether his earlier care had been of a different type? James thought so. At that stage the care had 'been done to him'. He now accepted that he had little energy reserves at that stage to help to make decisions or action care. Nevertheless, the nurse made a mental note to reassess the way the unit nurses communicated with the patient prior to carrying out each procedure.

James' dyspnoea was noticeably worse after he had completed his dressings or a short walk. At rest his respiratory rate fell from 28 to 24 breaths per minute. The sputum specimen had revealed staphylococcus aureus present, and given the proximity of his wounds, and his poor respiratory condition, James was started on a course of Cloxacillin added to his IV infusion line. Seated upright, with supporting pillows, James found breathing a little easier. This position was always assumed for controlled oxygen therapy (2 litres/minute through 28 per cent mix ventimask), prior to major wound toilet or chest physiotherapy. When the physiotherapist arrived the nurse showed James how to hold the pillow, covered in a sterile drape, against his chest dressing. Then when he coughed and tried to expectorate, the degree of discomfort might be limited. This measure proved only partially successful.

Deep breathing exercises were practised with James four or five times each day – in addition to the daily sessions provided by the physiotherapist. Frightened by the need for antibiotics, James was now eager to try and comply with the 5–10 minute sessions. He confided in the nurse that after starting work he had occasionally tried smoking cigarettes. This episode had 'put him off the habit for life'. The nurse told him this was especially wise given that he might need to undergo anaesthetic for future surgery.

James' sore bottom meanwhile was becoming an increasing problem. While no skin breakdown was in evidence, there was obvious redness, and James was becoming irritable about the need to sit upright for 'his chest's sake'. Various devices were employed, including an air flow mattress and seat cushion. After some experimentation James chose to spend a short period each shift kneeling in his high backed chair, leaning on the headrest which was in turn supported by a solid window ledge. Using this simple change of position James not only solved his own pressure problem by day, but was also able to view the comings and goings in the hospital ground outside. The monkey pole had proved too uncomfortable for James' hands at this stage – the high backed chair and a little imagination had proved superior.

After an initial flurry of visits during the shock period, James' parents' visits were now settling into a predictable routine. Mr Drew would visit in the afternoon and Mrs Drew in the early evening. James freely admitted that he found his mother's visits unproductive, she wanted to rush around his bed 'rearranging him' and at other times seemed tearful. The nurse asked James whether his experience of these visits was affected by how tired he was or by previous memories of his mother. James supposed that by early evening he was exhausted; earlier doses of analgesia for dressing changes had long worn off. In addition he was sometimes interrupted from watching television, one of the few distractions he was starting to enjoy again. James believed that his mother regretted that her only son had left home and was now reclaiming him.

At first, these sentiments seemed ungracious. James was seen to be taking an inappropriate stance about his grieving mother. Still, he had been through an ordeal and perhaps could be expected to act in a regressive, temporarily selfish manner. Further, visits did seem ill timed if James and his mother were to gain maximum support from one another. The nurse suggested to James that he might be better equipped to welcome his mother if he requested that his parents reverse their visiting times. In this way James would be less tired when he saw her and possibly still gaining the benefit of recent analgesia. His father's visits were always less fussy, with just a few practical points discussed. These would not interfere with television viewing, or over-tire James. Father and son might be distracted by programmes together. James thought this a worthwhile idea and agreed to propose it tactfully to his parents. As they were both retired now, it should not prove difficult to arrange.

Meanwhile, the nurse took the next visiting opportunity to ask how Mrs Drew thought her son's recovery was going. She thought that physically he was getting better, but that 'deep inside, there was still a great deal of hurt'. The nurse agreed that this was probably the case, and that such grief could affect patient and relatives for several months or more. This surprised Mrs Drew who thought that she was being really very strong for James. The nurse suggested that being very strong meant marshalling her resources, planning how to use them over a long period. Perhaps Mrs Drew was now in need of a short stock taking exercise? 'I've been going too fast', she said, 'my husband has said that I could burn myself out'.

The nurse counselled Mrs Drew on her efforts and how best to pace her support to James. She asked if James had seemed to react to her own tiredness, and she replied that she thought he had. She agreed to visit in the afternoons to please James. The nurse explained that this might do her good too. Seeing James less uncomfortable, looking more alert, would make her worry less. She could recharge her batteries and the nurses would be able to explain a little more about rehabilitation plans.

As the facial oedema subsided it became apparent that James would require one or more partial skin grafts to his right upper eyelid. To date, James had not recognised the importance of this. Yes, his eyes had watered, but he had been worried by his hands much more. Now, though, tissue contracture was causing his eyelid to retract and this placed his cornea in danger of ulceration. The nurse briefed the surgeon about James' perceived priorities and reported her observations about his right eye. She joined the surgeon as he explained the rationale of skin grafting to James, and noted his reactions to what the surgeon was saying. It was apparent that he was frightened by the idea of such surgery. That afternoon she persuaded Phillip, a twelve year old, previous burn victim, to visit James and explain about his experience of skin grafting. While Phillip had grafts to his arms, he remembered well the fear of an autograft being harvested from his thigh. He told James that it would be his leg that was more sore, 'the doctors are very nice to your burns'. The nurse confirmed that the donor site would be sore, but that analgesia would be available. Half consoled by this, James went to theatre and had his eyelid grafted. This graft took very well and James quickly sensed the better cover he had for his cornea.

James' physiotherapy has meanwhile been continuing. Healthy, granulating tissue was identified in some areas of his hands, but it was anticipated that grafts would soon be needed here too. James thought the polaroid pictures of his hands a perverse piece of nursing care, until the nurse was able to let him compare the degree of grip that he was now able to exert on a sponge ball with earlier pictures. Photographed against a white sheet, extension of his fingers was shown to be improving, albeit marginally.

It took some time for James to accept that keeping an audiotape diary of his experiences, specifically his opinion of his hands, would enable him to judge improvements. However, as the days slipped by, James began to realise that his memory was an unreliable record of his hands and their appearance. Comparing photographs, viewing his hands while listening to a tape of his previous observations, James had to admit that his palms were looking cleaner, even if he was disappointed with what they would do.

James continued to see Phillip on a once or twice weekly basis. Phillip had been in hospital several weeks longer than James and had undergone two operations post-burn already. He freely talked about missing a lot of next term's schooling so that suddenly James started to measure accurately what would be entailed in his own return to independence. After a visit from Phillip, James was noticeably quieter – one night he spoke of the bravery of the twelve year old and that which he would have to conjure up for the future.

James was now emotionally ready to learn how to handle other people and their reaction to him. Phillip had been positive, and now James' walks were proving less painful, leaving him less dyspnoeic. The nurse explained that most of the patients in the adjacent plastics ward had dealt with their own burn, scar or skin blemish. The relatives were sympathetic, even in awe of the determination shown by patients. For their first trip to the communal television room, James would be accompanied by his father and one nurse who would stay 'in the background'. James would sit at the back of the TV room, not that noticeable now that he had shed his IV infusion. It was planned that he would watch just one hour of a nature documentary. Before he set out, the nurse suggested ways of dealing with common enquiries about how he was recuperating and how long he had been in hospital. When he returned, triumphant, the nurse discussed the experience with him and his father, going over the anxieties, the difficult and the easier moments.

With the removal of the IV infusion, the treatment of chest infection and controlled use of oxygen, James was able to walk progressively further distances. Dressings were still painful but he no longer needed major analgesia. Exhausted at the end of a day of physiotherapy and increasing visits by workmates, James started to sleep more soundly. He could roll over free of constraining tubes, be these intravenous or the catheter (removed on his third day out of the shock room). Soon he would himself move to the plastics ward. There he would control daily hygiene, eating and elimination. He might still be circumspect about ordering food that needed cutting up, but the choice would be his. James was slowly moving to a stage of home-based care with intermittent hospital admissions for further reconstructive surgery. He would return to see the nurses of the burns unit and would perhaps encourage the patient that then occupied his old room. The nurses would expect that of him.

EVALUATION

Reviewing James' care in the post-shock period, the nurses were able to conclude that role transition in physical areas had been considerable. James had made the transition to oral fluids and in so doing re-established a large degree of homeostasis. As a result he had been able to discard his 'tubes' which in turn facilitated his increasing mobility. Hygiene standards had been satisfactorily maintained and James reported satisfaction with how his mouth now felt.

It was agreed that while the activity objectives had not been devised to deal with James' pain, this had in fact happened. Increased physiotherapy effort, freedom from restraints, meant that James was able to mobilise further. At the end of the day he could feel achievement in his efforts and went to bed ready to sleep. Improved quality of sleep led to increased exercise and pain tolerance the following day. Exercise and a personal determination to improve his hand function had proven a pain distraction. This seemed important at a time when the nurses had not actioned all of their pain control plans and when the physician had ended James' prescription for pethidine.

James' dyspnoea had proven a dual threat to his making a good recovery. Firstly, it could have occasioned a relapse in his condition, had physiotherapy and antibiotic therapy not been vigorously followed. Secondly, it could have undermined the success in his first exercises, which in turn might have hampered later motivation. The monitoring of James' respiratory state had been carefully performed, both in respect of balancing physiotherapy demand against rest and in terms of identifying complications such as infection and fluid overload.

Food intake had only improved once James had a comfortable mouth. After that, weight gain continued apace to the point where his dietary intake must be discussed again, relative to his energy needs and periodic boredom. James did not form a pressure sore, although it is suspected that he came perilously close during the opening days of the care plan.

Psychological and social problems show a more limited nursing success. In terms of communication roles, James did develop a real

34

partnership with both nurses and physiotherapist. The relationship with the consultant surgeon was rather more ambivalent, partly because of the latter's intermittent visits and perhaps because the nurses did not facilitate contact for the two parties as often as they might. Other communication roles were between James and his parents, and James and other patients on the ward. The most marked success had been with Phillip – a twelve year old who had shown surprising maturity. The nurses were grateful to Phillip for his therapeutic effect and determined that they should now review the criteria by which he was chosen as James' visitor. Had they chosen intuitively, or were there pointers by which a good visitor might be identified?

James' role relationship with his parents had proved a mixed bag. While no problems existed with reference to Mr Drew, the success of this partnership did tend to highlight the difficulties experienced between James and his mother. Both had entered the rehabilitation programme with a different definition of the situation. James had started from the perspective that his mother would use this as an opportunity to reset their relationship back to earlier years. Mrs Drew seemed to feel that James' personal contribution to his own rehabilitation would take a long time to develop. She appeared to confuse a motivating and supporting role with the more all embracing, and less helpful mothering role. The nurses' efforts to help establish a rehabilitation partnership had been moderately successful here. James was now welcoming his mother's interest and in turn Mrs Drew was pacing her interventions a little more sensitively. It remained to be seen whether these new roles could be sustained when James went home.

Finally, James had started to appreciate that recovery from a major burn was more of a marathon than a sprint. This had taken a long time to dawn on him, perhaps because he was still grieving the loss of his body image. It was difficult to judge whether patient education techniques had played a pre-eminent part in helping James to plan a long campaign. Equally influential may have been contact with other patients and the incidental discussions with his father.

JAMES DREW – REVIEW
QUESTIONS AND EXCERCISES

1. James, like many victims of trauma, proved to be a difficult patient to nurse. To what extent do you think his personality and his injury may have accounted for his behaviour?

2. The 'definition of the situation' was important throughout James' rehabilitation. What do you understand by this term? Who was involved in defining the situation?

3. If you were choosing a more experienced patient to visit James, what personal attributes and qualities would you look for within him or her?

4. To what extent is the surgeon at a disadvantage when trying to establish his therapeutic role with a patient such as James?

5. How does the burns unit environment facilitate or inhibit the nurses and patients ability to role take?

Exercises

For James, much of his adult male role was symbolically expressed through the power and function of his hands. They concerned him a great deal throughout the period of care. Draw up a list of reasons why you think this was. Then consider whether other patients (perhaps from a different background or gender) might react to burned hands in the same way. Compare your notes with a colleague.

CHAPTER FOUR

Graydon Powell: a teenager with cancer

In this second care study, we meet Graydon Powell, a very average fifteen year old with a very unaverage challenge. Graydon has developed Hodgkin's Lymphoma and this study will examine his problems and care during that early phase when his disease is staged and an initial course of radiotherapy started. As with other care studies in this volume, we shall be using the FANCAP assessment protocol espoused by Joan Riehl-Sisca. On this occasion, however, we shall be emphasising a very different practice consideration: that is, what should the nurse's role be at this point, and just how close a relationship should she form with the frightened Graydon Powell?

REVIEW OF THE SITUATION

Graydon comes from a suburban middle class family and attends the local comprehensive school. It is a time of considerable change for him and the emerging roles he wishes to play are not entirely clear. At once he wants to be an adult, grown up and sophisticated, but at the same time just how this is to be demonstrated isn't obvious either. Graydon experiences role confusion (Erikson, 1980) for he will soon be legally able to marry and start a family, but at the same time educational, family and financial considerations remind him of his dependent status. Body image changes are happening apace (Price, 1990) so he is regularly confronted by his forthcoming manhood, but he is still a teenage son too. Graydon's parents are very keen for him to do well at school, and they recognise the temptations of young adult life. It's apparent to Graydon that their advice is wise and he should be patient, persevering with his science studies.

During these formative teenage years his physical strength is important to him. His position in the school rugby team has gone unchallenged in previous seasons, and he has been relieved to get through the 'spotty phase of youth'. The world has been a rational, orderly place, with everyone's purpose (bar his) clearly defined. All that changed when he started to feel tired, lethargic and generally washed out. At first he put all this down to excessive study and a lack of fresh air. When he went jogging however, it was painfully obvious that his stamina was very depleted. Showering afterwards he noticed the pronounced 'bumps' in his axilla and the slight breathlessness which hadn't been there before. The bumps were painless, but obvious now his fingers crossed them.

He didn't want to burden his parents with worry so he arranged his own GP visit. Graydon's doctor examined him, took a thorough medical history and suggested he go into hospital, 'just to have a peep at some of the lumps'. When his parents found out about the planned admission they were upset that he hadn't felt able to share the worries earlier. Nevertheless, they have accompanied him to the hospital ward, where Graydon is to be assessed alongside the other adults that he feels are more natural companions than youngsters.

FANCAP ASSESSMENT

Graydon is assigned a primary nurse on this ward, and this is especially useful given that it specialises in medical investigations and, he soon realises, cancer treatment. As Nurse Booth begins to make her assessment, she realises that there are wider issues at stake than just Graydon's illness and his response to the same. Graydon is likely to be invited to become a patient for an indeterminate period of time, and his diagnosis may take a while to emerge. Further, this is a ward caring for patients with cancer so, even before diagnosis, Graydon will be confronted with his feelings about this word and all that he associates with it. Finally, Graydon has rapid role change in prospect. Assuming that Hodgkin's Lymphoma is confirmed, he will be asked to become an active participant in staging and then to make some very adult decisions with his parents and the staff concerning treatment. Hodgkin's Lymphoma may be treated by either radiotherapy, chemotherapy or a combination of both (Baez et al., 1991; Grodecki, 1991). Each carries with it sequelae that question Graydon's ability to adopt a positive and brave stance. She recalls that cure in this area is a relative term, with doctors talking about 5 and 10 year disease-free states (Bonadonna et al., 1988).

While technically useful, these terms do not seem calculated to imbue Graydon or his parents with a great sense of comfort or confidence. So, Graydon will be asked to adopt the role of survivor (Forbair *et al.*, 1986).

Because of all these considerations, Nurse Booth reviews the possible range of roles that she might play with Graydon during the forthcoming week. Initially she anticipates acting as a problem solver and teacher (Riehl-Sisca, 1989). She hopes that Graydon's self-esteem and youth will enable him to enter an active and honest relationship with her – during a period when physical health does not appear to be impaired to a major degree.

Fluids

Graydon shows no signs of being dehydrated, nor of the night sweats that can prove a significant feature in Hodgkin's Lymphoma (MacDonald, 1988). Graydon does not drink alcohol, so there has been no evidence of pain associated with intake of that to date. Given that Graydon has a healthy 2 to 3 litre daily intake of other fluids and a normal fluid balance (urine: nothing abnormal detected), she is relieved that if this is Hodgkin's Lymphoma, then there are no obvious category B symptoms to worry them. These are the additional problems recorded in the Ann Arbor staging protocol (cited in Carson and Callaghan, 1991), indicative of a poorer prognosis. As she assesses his fluid intake she notes his excellent state of oral hygiene and that his level of fluid intake may prove useful in the face of possible cancer therapy. If he is nauseated or tired later, fluid intake is likely to drop considerably.

It takes her several shifts to develop her appraisal of his mood state and how this has changed during his first hours on the ward. Nurse Booth does note though that Graydon's initial bright bravado has given way to a quiet contemplative manner, and this will have to be borne in mind as she cares for him during investigations and possible staging measures. For now, she concludes that Graydon is displaying a natural swing in his moods, facing as he does a daunting environment, with his parents unable always to be present.

Aeration

The first assessment of Graydon's physical respiration proves rather more worrying than his fluids one. Graydon clearly has a wheeze and this seems to be relatively constant at all phases of the respiratory cycle. There is no history of asthma in Graydon's family and he has not had a recent chest infection, so this is highlighted in Nurse Booth's report to the doctor. No sputum specimen is forthcoming and he is apyrexial, so she concludes there is at least a theoretical risk that Graydon may have mediastinal nodes or his respiratory tract affected by the condition. Graydon is pleased to tell her about his breathlessness of late, and the lost stamina, so she records these details and thanks him for his careful analysis of when the problem 'came on'. This is an opportunity to treat him as the adult he feels himself to be, and she enjoys helping him to map the particular problems out.

Through this discussion and a few supportive words concerning studies and the pressure of exams (she remembers her own) the nurse attempts to build a practical, 'let's examine the situation' relationship with Graydon. She anticipates the later problem-solving stage of her work, but for now has to accept that he is less forthcoming about some of his illness fears. He appears very factual about his condition and does not feel able to express his concerns, so at this stage she limits this assessment, in favour of building a first rapport.

Nutrition

Graydon has sustained a body weight which falls within his normal range for height, age and frame size, as well as what he has been accustomed to in the past. Nevertheless, he reports some fall off in his appetite and this seems to be linked with anxiety about his hospital stay and investigations. He has previously had a very healthy appetite but now seems distracted and more picky about his meals. The connection between appetite and anxiety is seized on by Nurse Booth who asks his parents just how Graydon has viewed his prospective admission to the ward. It becomes clear that their son is seen as a 'worrier, but very conscientious', so the nurse makes a mental note that assisting him to ventilate his feelings may be a developing problem. In any case, the relationship between Graydon and his parents seems both constructive and nurturant. They are concerned about his health and well-being, but understand too that he must be allowed freedom to cope in his own way too. The nurse has little time to examine the parent-teenager relationship much further, but she is initially impressed that each respects the other, and Graydon is seen as worthy of all the flexible support they can afford.

Communication

There are no obvious problems with Graydon's sense organs or his nervous system at this point. He wears spectacles to correct myopia and is well able to articulate his basic needs asking relevant questions concerning the daily ward routine. What is less clear is whether Graydon is suffering from information overload or sensory deprivation. Because Nurse Booth is unsure, she asks her associate to pay special attention to this area. The following day they conclude that Graydon's senses are fully stimulated by company and the television on the ward. He has not yet been deluged with information but this is anticipated as he undergoes a lymph node biopsy, blood sample examination, chest X-ray, lymphangiogram and bone marrow aspiration. It will therefore be important to prioritise the information given to Graydon and his parents, and to interpret the technical terminology with them. The role of interpreter and patient advocate are well known to both the nurses.

Graydon's primary nurse is mindful that she still has no real impression of his perception of cancer or what the investigations may mean. She is aware too that 'staging' is an alien concept to him, employing a series of procedures that may seem gratuitously painful or frightening. For that reason she decides quickly that some of these details will have to be discussed with Graydon's parents first. By this means she hopes to negotiate a second supportive filter, by which Graydon may come to understand what is being planned, gradually. If she does this, it must be tactfully handled, for she is aware that she is developing a trust relationship with Graydon too.

Activity

Despite Graydon's recent lack of stamina, he moves around the ward with ease and appears to sleep soundly at night. Indeed, his comparative fitness is in stark contrast to some of the more debilitated and fatigued patients receiving care. Because of this, some of the other nurses have involved Graydon in minor ward chores. Through this activity, Graydon gets to know his patient colleagues and to form useful relationships with some of the younger ward community members. Less constructive is the attention shown by Graydon to various members of staff. There are times when he follows nurses around, seeking information about the ward and the general treatments they use. During a report handover, Nurse Booth reports this observation and it's agreed that he is probably trying to find out more about cancer, and the ward, while distancing all such threats from his own person.

This seems a familar ploy to the nurse, but she remembers too that she must establish an honest, clear communication channel, with mutual expectations between Graydon and herself. If he gleans his interpretation of events from diverse sources, it (a) may be very confused and (b) may cause anxiety to others. All wards incorporate an unofficial information grapevine, and information is given as well as received, however accurate or inappropriate.

Pain

Graydon's enlarged axillary lymph glands are painless, and his slight wheeze in the chest equally so. It is true, though, that he must ancticipate some discomfort if his investigations go on to include a bone marrow aspiration as well as the lymph gland biopsy. Lymphangiograms and blood sample collection too may be associated with minor pain. Nurse Booth concludes from Graydon's surreptitious information gathering that he is indeed fearful of what might happen (emotional pain). This is a common problem among patients faced with the prospect of cancer (Bramwell, 1989), but it will not be sufficient to leave it recorded just at this level. She resolves to discover just what Graydon fears most, and to use this where possible to plan an education programme that parallels his potential staging, and precedes any necessary treatment. This will be a major part of her problem-solving and teaching roles.

NURSING DIAGNOSIS

Because Graydon's diagnosis and possible treatment plans are initially very open-ended, it is only possible to be very tentative about his nursing diagnosis at this stage. Nurse Booth appreciates that Graydon does not yet have a clear patient role and he and they are going through a period of negotiating what their relationship will be like. Making notes in his folder prior to a more formal care plan, she attempts to work out what the problems are likely to be (see Figure 4.1). For this nurse, spider diagrams often clarify relationships and roles. She finds them useful after a fairly detailed but often piecemeal assessment. On this occasion she is helped to conclude several points which will help her to build a care plan.

First, Graydon has brought some of his role confusion into hospital. He is being nursed on an adult ward but he's not perhaps

Figure 4.1

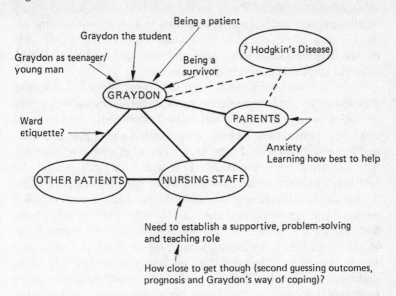

completely an adult yet. This has meant he is still learning the right ways to handle the ward and its etiquette. In a very real sense then, Graydon needs help to become socialised into the ward community. This is not a coercive venture, but simply a need if he is to establish a good relationship with those others who share the environment. This is an especially prominent problem when she reviews information on the ward, and how Graydon seeks to use it to assuage some hidden anxieties. Similarly, this applies to how Graydon meets and co-operates with the nurses and doctors who seek to help him. Graydon is a human being trying to make sense of his worth, his achievements and worries, so it is important not to damage his self-esteem unnecessarily now. Nevertheless, she sees the working out of a professional relationship as being key to all his other therapy and counselling. Callery and Smith (1991) have discussed the stages of a relationship in terms of role and she thankfully recalls their points about parental uncertainty over role too. Even more germane were some points she remembered concerning mutual relationships (Morse, 1991). Four types of relationship exist and Graydon's circumstances fitted more than one. In terms of the potentially limited time in hospital spent now, their relationship could be 'clinical'. The role relationship could be courteous but quite super-ficial. Against this, it could be seen as 'therapeutic'. In this instance, the ward sister expected her to view Graydon first within the patient role and only secondarily as a person with a life outside. Graydon's needs however might through diagnosis and treatment become far more taxing. She might have to negotiate a 'connected' relationship in which she acted as Graydon's advocate, seeking to buffer him from the unpleasant aspects of treatment.

So far, she was happy and familiar with these role needs, but there was also a further factor to take into account. Graydon was a very appealing patient, intelligent and helpful where he thought he could help. Should he receive a cancer diagnosis and a poor prognosis, she and her colleagues would have to monitor whether the relationship was becoming 'over involved'. This was a difficult subject for Graydon's primary nurse. Not wishing to limit her support under frightening circumstances she nevertheless had to reserve some emotional energy and commitment for the other patients in her care, and indeed for herself if she was not to become burned out (McConnell, 1982). It was with some misgivings that she concluded she must spell out the limitations on how she saw her care being delivered, to Graydon and his parents. It would be important to negotiate, but she had to review her commitments to the other patients and junior nurses as well.

Some of the other role problems and needs seemed a little less daunting after that. She recalled that Graydon was a student and that he might need help to pace his studies, against hospital care and possible future treatment. She remembered too he was accommodating role change, becoming a patient and trying to make sense of hospital jargon and departmental procedures. She could not forget Graydon's pleasant parents, who appeared anxious to work out just how they might assist their son best. There would be a need to teach them much of what was proceeding and then to help them to value their son's personal coping styles. At last she was ready to negotiate a care plan with Graydon and his parents. Right now it would emphasise the psychological and social needs of Graydon, but later radiotherapy or cytotoxic chemotherapy might pose additional, physical challenges (see care plan in Table 4.1).

CARE IN ACTION

During the following days, Graydon undergoes a series of investigations as anticipated. In addition to a chest X-ray being performed, blood samples are taken and one of his enlarged axillary lymph nodes is biopsed. The tissue is sent to the hospital laboratory for histological examination. Graydon found the whole experience understandably distressing, but pain levels minimal. In fact, the most irritating aspect of it was the way the sutures pulled when he raised his arm afterwards. His primary nurse shows him a range of physical exercises to keep his shoulder mobile at this time, and promises that the sutures will be removed as soon as the wound has healed about five days later. The first physical investigations have served to make the threat of cancer very real to Graydon, and during an evening discussion with Nurse Booth and his parents, he admits that he is scared. It is not so much the disease ('you can't see that, other than through little lumps'), more the fact that some other patients with confirmed Hodgkin's Disease seem to have their 'tummies cut open'. Nurse Booth realises that Graydon is referring to a staging laparotomy and is pleased to tell him a little bit more about staging and why different patients have different things planned for them. She explains that this operation is done to look for the disease in the abdomen where there is good indication it has spread that far, and it is thought that more accurate information will help the doctor to decide on treatment. It does not feature in every patient's circumstance, and a lymphangiogram (an X-ray picture of his glands, such as those in his arm pits and groin) and bone marrow aspiration (to see if there is disease in his blood-making areas) are earlier, sometimes sufficient investigations. Staging is about mapping out the progress of the disease, so the best treatment can be used to attack tumour cells and help the patient get better.

Afterwards, she quickly reviews with Graydon's parents what they thought his feelings were about her summary. She realises there was a lot of technical information involved, and was keen to clarify that, without simplifying it to a point where she appeared to patronise Graydon. They seemed pleased with her efforts, and confirmed he did indeed look relieved at what she had said. As she went away to update the care plan and report to her associate nurses, she reflected that she was a learner too. Graydon's parents were her teachers, acquainting her with the niceties of how Graydon interpreted events. She felt confident that in return they had felt able to contribute to Graydon's total package of care. Helping the nurse, helped Graydon as well.

The sequence of major and minor investigations, physical examinations and care explanations quickly started to fill the following days. The discussion about patient role took a lot of tactful couching over three informal chats, but she did explain how slowly all would become clearer, and the nurses would help him to plan what to do

Table 4.1 *Graydon Powell: initial care plan*

Nursing diagnosis	Goal	Nursing interventions
Aeration problems		
1a Graydon has problems directly expressing his fears about his health and the investigations	With our help, Graydon will feel confident to ask searching questions and express his feelings about what is happening	1. Explore further with his parents, Graydon's preferred coping strategies 2. Establish just how much Graydon currently seeks to share about his worries 3. Set aside a time each evening shift (quieter then) when we will review the day with him (facilitate opportunity to express misgivings) 4. Assure Graydon that his mood may swing back and forth but he is still valued and won't be criticised if he feels angry or tearful 5. Review whether Graydon gets on better with me or my associate nurses – build a plan accordingly
Nutrition problems		
2a Graydon's parents are seeking a new role, nurturing their son more expertly during uncertainty	Through education and discussion, Graydon's parents will learn a new array of skills to cope with Graydon's moods, and potentially ill body	1. Review with them the common fears we understand they may have at present 2. Invite them to reflect how they see the role of their family being affected by Graydon's illness 3. Summarise same and highlight positive examples of how other parents have successfully coped

4. Introduce parents to the hospital family support group co-ordinator
5. Agree with them what they would like to do in the eventuality that Graydon requires cancer treatment

---

| 2b Graydon's dietary intake has fallen and potential treatment will suppress appetite, and induce nausea and vomiting | Graydon will feel happy to eat a high protein, well balanced diet prophylactic against future treatment or disease state | 1. Brief Graydon on the need for a balanced diet, namely (i) stress, (ii) studying, (iii) possible diagnosis and (iv) potential treatment
2. Assist him in selecting foods and supplements which tempt his appetite
3. Monitor body weight and dietary intake daily
4. Review oral hygiene state and fluid balance in anticipation of future possible treatment |

Communication problems

| 3a Graydon's patient role is confused (unclear diagnosis – limbo effect) | Graydon will be assisted with his parents to map out possible future courses of action appropriate to diagnosis, treatment and his coping style | 1. Interview parents about family experience/perceptions of hospital, cancer and cancer treatment
2. Establish more detail about Graydon's way of coping
3. Create (initially with parents) some scenarios and response options. These to include radiotherapy, cytotoxic chemotherapy and a combination therapy
4. Agree with Graydon the speed and volume of information he wants to handle. Does he have a preferred 'interpreter'? |

| 3b Graydon doesn't understand the investigations and possible staging protocol | Graydon will achieve informed consent to the procedures (in concert with his parents) | 1. Establish the sequence of investigations to be done
2. Arrange regular briefings on the next, linking same to projected time of results and significance with reference to treating Graydon accurately and sensitively |

47

3. Regularly (every third day) review patient and parent response to same, in order to answer questions about family coping strategies

Activity problems

4a Graydon is attempting to learn about potential problems/diagnosis from other patients (risk of further confusion of roles – distress to Graydon and others)	Graydon will feel comfortable discussing his worries with his primary nurse or other staff member	1. Explore with Graydon the settling-in relationship with patients (for example, with reference to their illnesses and stages of care avoiding breach of medical confidence points) 2. Review patient role *vis-à-vis* anxiety and unclear diagnosis in order to remain empathetic to Graydon 3. Outline the possible distorted effects of rumour grapevine 4. Agree avenues of free information – assuring him of openness
4b Graydon in assisting nurses can become confused concerning patient versus helper role	Graydon will be helped to value the contributions he makes, but to separate out time for queries about treatment (with the nurse)	1. Establish private time to discuss his fears with him 2. Reward his enthusiasm to help, but agree better times to discuss sensitive information

Pain problems

5a Graydon's role may change rapidly as he is diagnosed and treated. Grief may increase his demands upon primary nurse	Graydon will be assured of constructive and thoughtful support, shared between the nurses and his parents' responsibility	1. Brief Graydon's parents about teamwork approach to care 2. Explain ideas about a controlled and therefore sustainable commitment (burn out can affect parents too) 3. Agree areas where parents and nurses will specialise care input

| 5b Potential for physical pain associated with investigations | Physical pain will be anticipated, assessed and controlled through negotiation with Graydon | 1. Brief Graydon on all procedures
2. Reassure him about pain relief measures
3. Monitor his level of comfort
4. Adjust his position/ support with him as necessary
5. Administer appropriate prescribed analgesia, after proper assessment of patient need |

about his feelings and future possible trips to hospital. During the evening she found it important to reread notes on coping (Lazarus and Folkman, 1984; Benner and Wrubel, 1989) and to refer to previous care studies she had completed during her oncology nursing course. It was sad but true, she had always found it most difficult to retain and use the material on the psychological aspects of cancer.

When the news came back that Graydon did indeed have Hodgkin's Lymphoma, it neither surprised this nurse nor relieved her completely of her stress in looking after Graydon and his parents. Now, it was obvious her role would change, but the challenge was still considerable. There was a known 'enemy' and it was important to measure its strength and position. The war-like analogy had been useful before, many times, so that's where she started now. The consultant sat down with Graydon separately to tell him the news, advising him he was a very mature teenager who deserved his own time and a frank explanation. At the same time, Nurse Booth explained the diagnosis and staging to Graydon's mother and father. It would then be a further hour later before she joined parents and son at the bedside to explore how the family's own private review of the situation had gone.

Previous experience with families had taught her that it was impossible to predict how they might react to confirmed diagnosis, even if nurse and doctor had provided a graded explanation of possibilities beforehand. Her role now therefore was to listen, to reassess family feelings, values, their motivation towards staging and treatment. It came as a welcome relief when she discovered that the previously clear and balanced family relationships stood them in good stead to report their convictions now. Graydon was tearful, his mother holding his hand tightly as his father explained that they were going to 'tackle this thing sensibly, and be brave about it all'.

Staging procedures followed and Graydon started, albeit hesitantly, to open his textbooks alongside trips to the X-ray department (lymphangiogram) and minor operations suite where a bone marrow aspiration was completed. For most of these procedures, Graydon was accompanied by Nurse Booth and a very keen and supportive student nurse. Then, each evening Graydon's nurse briefed his parents on progress, when they visited after work. The sum of all the staging investigations revealed that Graydon had a stage 2a tumour, with lymph nodes in his axilla and mediastimum affected. This accounted for his chesty condition. When the doctor explained this to the family he was able to offer them a relatively optimistic prognosis. Seven out of ten people with this sort of lymphoma, at this stage, might look forward to being disease free in ten years time. Nevertheless, it was now important to arrange a course of radiotherapy – if progress was to be brisk.

RADIOTHERAPY TREATMENT

In Graydon's case, the course of treatment chosen consisted of a programme (fractionated) of extended field external radiotherapy. This was to be delivered over a mantle area (affecting neck, upper chest, both axilla and the mediastinal regions) so as to maximise the opportunity to destroy tumour cells while minimising the side effects that Graydon would have to face. The purpose of fractional doses was well understood by Nurse Booth and her student companion, but she appreciated that it was new to her patient and his family. Further, Graydon would be introduced to a new department of the hospital, and its attendant staff (radiotherapists). This placed a focus of treatment outside the ward, while the focus of care remained predominantly within it. Graydon would spend comparatively short periods of time first in the radiotherapy simulator room, and the treatment suite itself, before bringing back his fears and any physical side effects for care and support on the ward.

Communication within the hospital has always been good, but still, she reminds her associate nurses that there is here a potential for mismatched information and patient distress. Graydon could feel that the nurses don't completely appreciate his departmental experiences, or that he may view the therapists as dispassionate and insensitive to his concerns. Accordingly, the nurse once again resorts to a spider diagram to explain his needs, and the relevant caring roles, to the attendant student nurse (Figure 4.2). Discussion among the nurses centres upon whether Graydon and his parents have moved sufficiently far in response to the situation, to really fulfil the new role in her diagram. It's agreed that they all display an open interest in how radiotherapy helps, and how the tiredness and redness of Graydon's skin is minimised by the doses being 'split up'. So it is concluded that they are fully fledged in their learning role, having dealt with the first flood of grief that accompanied the staging process. Less consensus of opinion exists though on whether Graydon has really become a copee. It is evident from his closer reliance recently on his parents that he looks for coping examples from them. There is less evidence that he has understood his own irritable feelings which occasionally get displayed on the ward. In

Figure 4.2

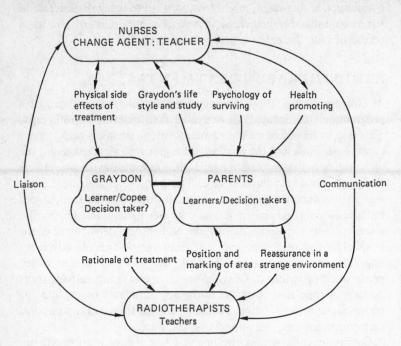

the meantime, Graydon's parents have approached their discussions with the radiotherapists very much as decision takers. They often relay ideas back to Graydon, and embellish his questions to the therapist with their own needs to understand the scientific aspects of what is happening.

Reluctantly, the nurses conclude that the treatment protocol is proceeding ahead, there is a measured urgency to do so, and as a result they must adopt a mix of teacher and change agent roles promptly. The teaching aspect of their role will address how to look after Graydon's radiotherapy-treated body areas (skin care), rest in response to tiredness and planned limited periods of study. Graydon is anxious not to fall behind so his mother volunteers to read the necessary school work with him, so that discussion of topics can be both his distractor from treatment and a less onerous form of revision. Other aspects of the teaching role for the nurses will be concerned with maintaining intake of a nutritious diet, responding to subsequent opportunistic infections and helping Graydon to balance a need for exercise and relaxation (he is keen to consider playing rugby in due course). The change agent role is taken almost exclusively by Nurse Booth. She recognises that he will need assistance to reflect on his feelings of vulnerability, of being an insecure survivor, and that this will be critical if he is to sustain the excellent family relationships that already exist. The period of Graydon's course of radiotherapy is limited to a few weeks, so she assigns her associate nurses the role of teaching and takes the change agent responsibilities herself. Both carers will play a role in physical care and in addressing support to Graydon's mother and father.

Reviewing her notes on how closely to get involved with Graydon, she is pleased to rediscover that the change agent role really does help sort this out. To be a change agent, helping Graydon to take responsibility for his own care, feelings and the handling of other's enquiries, she could not easily adopt an over-involved relationship stance. Her role will be to counsel Graydon, acting as a catalyst, helping him to put his future symptom-free state into some sort of order. It is a daunting challenge, but she hopes to help him build a live life (sensibly) to the full philosophy. In one as young as Graydon, philosophising about how he wants to live may not have been prominent before. Now, confronted with a realistic risk of disease recurrence, regular medical review, he needs help to discover the positive aspects of his studies, his family and his health. During the next four weeks she introduces the topic of feelings, confidence and coping, into discussions on his studies and sport. She takes an active interest in how he has progressed with his reading and together they share memories of just how hard it can be to assign time to each area of revision. Life can be hard, Graydon says, and she realises this reflects not just his exam preparation but response to illness too. Examining this down to earth, pragmatic approach, she is able to introduce the idea of 'thinking work, feeling work'. These both play a part in life and it is good to give them time, otherwise he will find it hard to help his parents, who seek to understand just how he feels. Sharing the work, like the revision he has shared with his mother, seems a good way to get the best help when he needs it, but privacy when he doesn't. After the school exams, Graydon offers, the three of them plan a short holiday in Cornwall. If he is well enough he wants to do some more thinking then, but to have fun as well. She congratulates him on the plan, saying what a good idea it seems.

EVALUATION

It was several days after Graydon left hospital, his course of radiotherapy complete, that his primary nurse and two of her associates found time to evaluate his care fully. In the meantime she had provided his community care team with some first impressions of his outstanding needs and the state of Graydon and his parents' relationship. His role as survivor and 'treatment veteran' (as he rather overstated it) was not yet fully established but he had made imaginative steps when she recalled his rather private way of coping when he first was admitted to hospital. Like many of their conversations it started with expressions of frustration. Patients were treated and cared for in hospitals under such pressure that care was dictated by treatment schedules rather than patient need. Graydon had limited time to acclimatise to his patient role and then his survivor status. The nurses had even less time to establish the sort of rapport so critical to good quality care.

They knew that the move to change agent was a hurried role development for them, and that copee was also dictated by considerations beyond Graydon's circumstances. Nevertheless, these major constraints apart he had made a balanced progress. Graydon had established a good working relationship with the nurses and this had been considerably aided by the mature and calm response of his parents. In many respects, their early interpretation of their son's mood, level of insight and motivation had enabled the nurses to move forward with new teaching and counselling at a pace which this apart could seem almost breakneck.

In particular, the nurses congratulated themselves that they had used the period of investigations and then staging to build the relationship with Graydon. It was a pro-active piece of care because they had commenced a useful counselling relationship and helped him to realise the professional boundaries of support even against the backdrop of diagnosis and threatening procedures. One of the associate nurses had misgivings about this, wondering whether the nurse should in fact be quite so explicit about explaining role relationships, the level and type of commitment that could be expected from the nurses at different stages of an illness. The others were less disturbed by the approach, feeling that while it must have seemed strange initially, it did pay dividends as Graydon was assisted to deal with his own feelings, coping strategies and health care thereafter. There was a real risk that anxiety, fear and an overwhelming need (on the part of the nurse) to alleviate these patient emotions totally, could result in an over-involved care relationship. This might then have complicated the role to be played by Graydon's parents, post his discharge from hospital. They all agreed that a nurse had to examine her resources of energy, patience, compassion, and ask if the role of the nurse during diagnosis, staging and early treatment permitted their fullest use. Above and beyond the needs of other patients, Graydon's illness career would change, and he would need different role relationships at different times. No stage was mutually exclusive, the role they played now would have a significant effect upon their future caring roles.

Following this, the nurses asked themselves the question: did we support the family as a whole? On balance they felt that they did, negotiating just what would be especially useful to each of them early on. It was this family dimension of care that had probably afforded some of their success. No two cancer sufferers are alike, and the course and stage of Hodgkin's Lymphoma is not the sole indicator of how nurses should construct their patient care roles. It would have been easy to adopt a disease-dictated, unreflective pattern of care for 'Hodgkin's sufferers', but this would have been unsubtle, if not dangerous to Graydon. Only by adjusting care, advice and answers to questions, so as to reflect Graydon's personality, age, social and family circumstances, could the right relationship be arrived at so early on. Graydon would return to the hospital again and again for check-ups if nothing else. It had to be right.

Graydon's physical care was adjudged to have been a considerable success. He had achieved an uncomplicated course of treatment, the side effects of radiotherapy being limited to a minor degree of skin erythema and a diminished intake of food during the third week of the protocol. There had been no need to adjust or delay his course of radiotherapy and gradually his energy levels were beginning to rise during the final week of hospitalisation. It was pointed out to him that he could feel below par for many weeks to come, and he should gradually increase his exercise – but that this notwithstanding, he should soon be feeling fit once more.

When the nurses came to summarise, reviewing their own and the family's changing role, they decided that a shift in the positive direction had occurred. Graydon had moved from someone seeking help with a problem, becoming a co-operative, even an appreciative care receiver. He had listened to the advice on how he might best assist the nurses and had gone on to become a learner and, to a limited level, finally a copee. His parents meanwhile had progressed further, becoming active in his care within the radiotherapy department and in liaising with his General Practitioner (as both doers and advocates). The nursing element (Nurse Booth and associate nurses) had fulfilled multiple roles with varying degrees of success. As problem solvers they had been expert, care giving and teaching moderately well, while as a change agent Nurse Booth felt she had made reasonable first steps. Only the months ahead, and Graydon's outpatient clinic role, would determine whether she had really achieved a considerable success. She noted the date of Graydon's Out Patient Appointment in her diary and made a note to see him then if she possibly could. She was curious to learn of his progress, and to evaluate this last and most taxing of care roles.

GRAYDON POWELL – REVISION QUESTIONS AND EXERCISES

1. Graydon Powell's lack of a definitive diagnosis slowed down the development of patient and nursing roles. Read back over the study and try to analyse just why this was? (Hint: You may wish to talk about patient motivation, the ethics of information control or the need to treat Graydon as a family member.)

2. Graydon was fifteen years old. This has a significant part to play in his readiness to accept new roles. Try to suggest just why this may be?

3. The nurse found her role as change agent the most taxing. For her this involved assisting Graydon to respond to his own problems, to reflect on his own solutions. It involved counselling Graydon, but could have involved other facets too. Can you suggest what these could have been? (Hint: What about establishing a personal discipline framework? Graydon may need to cope with periods when he feels sorry for himself.)

4. Cancer produces a fairly well documented reaction of fear among the general public. This is perhaps made more pervasive by poorly represented statistics on morbidity and mortality of different tumours. What role does the nurse have, promoting a more positive first public response?

5. The nurses complained about their multiple roles, driven by treatment protocols and the demand for limited hospital resources. What sort of additional education, skill enhancement, do you think you would need to fulfil such a multifaceted nursing role?

6. Graydon's nurse was quite explicit about adopting certain roles, and asking associates to adopt others. Her use of spider diagrams helped in this. To what extent do you think adopting roles consciously in this way, could improve care for Graydon?

Exercises

This care study (unlike some others within this book) has emphasised the psycho-social care of a patient during an anxiety provoking episode in his life. These exercises build upon that issue.

Critical incident analysis

Working first individually and then with close colleagues in a group, it is possible to share in a safe way, our experiences of dealing with a critical incident and the way it affected our role or roles. Because you choose the incident, and the amount that you divulge about it, there should be only a minimal amount of stress linked to this exercise. So, review your nursing (or if you feel confident) your social life to pick out an incident that was important for you and the role that you play. That incident could be a salutory lesson learned, or something you feel you got especially right. It could have been an accident, or a Eureka moment, when theory and practice suddenly came together.

Make some brief notes about it, adding details about the role or roles affected. Remember, the incident could have enhanced your role or detracted from it. Once you have done this, join with your other group members to share your experiences. As a protocol, everyone should agree that discussion should centre upon how the incident made you feel *vis à-vis* your own roles – and not upon how your colleague coped. We suggest you ask an experienced nurse teacher or other facilitator to assist in this process. When you have shared these experiences and feelings, consider these questions:

Are there any dominant factors which can serve to force or encourage nurses into new roles?
If so, how should nurses prepare to meet the challenge?

What if . . .?

Another useful exercise is to imagine what would be the result if historically a different course of events were to have happened. Historians, for instance, have pondered how the world would be if

Britain had been on the losing side in World War 2. In this exercise we are going to look at a different course of events for Graydon, and ask you to imagine how this would affect the nurse's roles.

Imagine that Graydon's investigations reveal that in fact he has an advanced stage of Hodgkin's Lymphoma, and that the tumour cells have spread to his abdominal organs. How would the nurse's roles differ now?

Devise your own personal ideas on this and then use the Riehl list of nursing roles to formulate some fuller ideas on the same with a group of colleagues.

CHAPTER FIVE

Irene Watkins: the asthmatic lady

INTRODUCTION

The studies we have so far considered have featured, in hospital, relatively acute situations. But of course the Riehl Interaction Model is equally applicable in more chronic circumstances, and as here, with Mrs Irene Watkins, within the community. By considering Irene's story, you should be able to reflect upon the different care plan formats that are necessitated by different settings. We hope too that you will reflect upon the role implications of chronic, yet intermittent illness, both for the patient and the community nurse who supports her. Irene's circumstances are by no means unique. She is a divorcee, aged 51 who along with two and a half million other British people, suffer from asthma. Like many of these patients, Irene frequently becomes fed up with coping with her nagging problem, and she resents the treatment upon which she relies. Irene has had several decades to accommodate a patient role which features independent coping. Her extrinisic asthma was diagnosed when she was still a teenager, but she has only partially adapted to the role of pro-active person. There has been only marginal adjustment of her lifestyle to deal actively with the psychological and social aspects of her problem.

REVIEW OF THE SITUATION

Irene lives in a modest, and rather elderly terraced house in the inner part of a northern city. She works as a junior school teacher, and previous commitments to looking after her frail mother, as well as cash flow problems after the divorce, have meant she cannot afford to move home. Despite these problems she has tried to remain cheerful, throwing a lot of energy into her work with disadvantaged school children. Irene's asthma has been diagnosed as extrinsic (Barnes, 1988; Paul and Fafoglia, 1988), but it is recognised that the attacks are exacerbated when she becomes highly stressed, or over-worked (Brucia *et al.*, 1987). In Irene's case, multiple allergens trigger off her asthma attacks. The principal ones are house dust (and the attendant mites), chalk dust (from her place of work), some tree pollens and (she thinks), the damp mould which affects some parts of her mother's home (Kersten, 1989). These substances precipitate a hypersensitive reaction within her lungs, and this results in the bronchospasm, narrowing of bronchial passage ways and wheezing which Irene refers to as her 'damned weak chest'. During recent winter months she has noticed that the weakness of her chest has permitted chest infections to take hold that much more quickly. She has suffered two recent winter episodes when she has become temporarily house-bound, and only slowly recovered from influenza. To date, hospital admission for acute exacerbations of her asthma have been comparatively rare. The last of these was nearly three years ago, when she was admitted as an emergency, following her efforts to tame her overgrown garden one summer.

Irene had a fairly good working relationship with her community nurse, Denise Cooper, whom she saw either at the local group practice or occasionally at school (where Denise has two youngsters attending class). Still, it's a strangely one-sided relationship at times, because despite being intelligent, and often quite well organised, Irene does seem to expect Denise to direct what should be done about her periodic asthma problems. This sort of reluctance to take decisions has been documented with a range of patients (Waterworth and Luker, 1990), but it nonetheless worries the nurse as asthma problems are often amenable to the patient's own control measures. It requires only that the patient adopt a decision-making role, and this she feels Irene is well able to do.

Normally, given that Irene is not currently faced with a physical crisis, Denise could not contemplate stopping to re-explore this one of many patients' asthma problems. On this day, however, she has spent a lot of time pondering how Irene might be helped to forestall asthma attacks even more effectively. She has noticed how drawn and tired Irene is looking at school, so she concludes it would not hurt to visit her and review her current treatment and coping strategies.

FANCAP ASSESSMENT

Denise Cooper's assessment of Irene's situation benefits from a long-standing relationship between them. She felt confident about exploring the asthma dilemma, because her role as investigator and health promoter was well understood by Irene. This was useful, as the FANCAP assessment system was new to her, and she would need to consider each of her patient's needs very carefully.

Fluids

In the conventional, physiological sense, Irene had no problems either with her fluid intake or her fluid balance. The asthma attacks had not severely limited her intake of beverages, and the regular school meal breaks and recesses enabled her to drink a welcome cup of coffee. Regarding her situation, however, her role relationships with others, there was considerable change under way. Four months earlier Irene finally lost her mother after a long-standing cancer illness. She was clearly distressed by the loss, and sensibly took time off work to deal with her grief. As her father died many years earlier, and she was an only child, this has left her largely alone. Her work (complicated by recent school re-organisation) has further marginalised her existence, demanding that she put extra hours of marking and lesson preparation in, so as to maintain her high standards of practice. Work, which had once proven a solace post divorce, was now an additional burden – and Denise Cooper felt that Irene was very much at a crossroads.

Aeration

Irene's respiratory condition had gradually deteriorated over a number of years. At school she had been a wheezy athlete of limited ability, who was able to take part as long as her mother never found out, and her teacher was feeling adventurous. The use of spinhalers was to prove a godsend to her, as now she could, in adult years, administer useful drugs, direct to the source of the problem. Denise asked Irene to show her the asthma drugs she currently took. These were all inhaled, and consisted of Sodium Cromoglycate 20 mg (Intal) four times a day, Beclomethasone 250 mcg (Becloforte) twice a day (at least, during high pollen count periods, or when she'd suffered winter colds) and Salbutamol 100 mcg (Ventolin) used as her 'fire engine drug' when she had an attack. Denise noted the combination and timing of the drugs, and jotted these down to check against Group Practice records. She was eager to explore when the protocol had been arranged, and asked Irene how often she saw her GP. Irene's reply was vague. At one time it had been six monthly, but she could not recall visiting her during the past year.

Next, Irene was asked to just run through her technique for taking her drugs. It was possible that she was self-administering only a part of the dose, owing to faulty practice. Watching Irene use the inhaler, Denise was satisfied that she could indeed use these and spinhalers efficiently, but she wondered whether such attention to detail was always evident when she wasn't being observed, or operating in calm conditions. Enquiries about whether she had spotted any problems or irritations in taking the drugs, drew almost a blank. It took a little encouragement to have Irene admit she felt that her airways got awfully dried out with the Intal powder. Gentle encouragement also enabled her to concede that she took her medicines in private while she was at school. It was not that the other teachers didn't know she was an asthmatic, rather that she disliked sharing how much she relied upon her medication. Richardson (1991) has explored both these psycho-social and the physical challenges of adults dealing with chronic asthma. In her study, patients felt that their career and employment prospects were affected by the condition and that a significant number of respondents were embarrassed by asthma symptoms or the need to take medication in public. Patients felt angry, frustrated and resentful at having to try and control allergens, their environment, in an effort to limit attacks and fend off respiratory infections.

To Denise Cooper this research seemed very relevant. Irene was experiencing work pressure to adapt to change, just at a time when she felt emotionally and physically vulnerable. It seemed likely that there were few people to whom she could ventilate her feelings of anger and loss. This additional stressor might very likely exacerbate her respiratory condition. Watching Irene give her account of events and feelings, it was evident that she maintained little eye contact when she tried to express her hurt. Nurse Cooper concluded that over many decades Irene may have been helped to inhale her medication quite satisfactorily, but the meaning of this illness, and her emotional responses, had really not been attended to fully.

Nutrition

Irene was 21 pounds overweight for her height and frame size, and this was noted against her brief comments about exercise. She had a preponderance of convenience food to eat, and relied upon her microwave oven at home, and school dinners at work, where she helped 'keep an eye on the lunch proceedings'. Denise at this stage was not so concerned as to ask Irene to give a detailed dietary breakdown, but she did ask her to consider the balance between protein and carbohydrate intake, calories and exercise, as all were important if she was to fight infection and limit the demands being made upon her chest. Later, it would be important to return to the issue of diet, because if Irene was to be helped to take more exercise, she would need to consider how this was best fuelled.

On the nurturing side of nutrition, Irene was clearly inadequately supported. Her social support network consisted of two teacher acquaintances, and an old school friend she occasionally visited for weekends. It was remarked that all her friends were married, with families, so she felt uncomfortable making too many demands upon their time. Up until now, she had not stopped to map out just how limited her social circle was, and she admitted to feeling disappointed in herself that she had allowed things to get to this state of affairs. Denise was eager to ressure Irene that circumstances had not helped her recently, and she shouldn't take a wholly negative view of herself. Her mother's care and the additional school work had severely limited opportunities, but she was right, now might be the time to plan a new pattern of friendships.

Communication

All of this led naturally enough into a review of Irene's communication with others, and, more specifically, what her perceptions and interpretation of her situation were. It had been Denise's repeated experience that physical problems or disease in themselves did not predict just how well a patient would cope. Far more instructive was the patient's 'attitude of mind' – and this seemed significant time and again with patients dealing with long-term health deficits. Patients had a 'norm', an expectation of how they lived their lives, and how they would relate to other people. This included their contact with health care staff, and the degree to which it was insulted by disease could foretell just how they might cope. Health visitors and others have frequently had to deal with the unique norms of their clients (Cowley, 1991), so this wasn't new to Denise, nor unique to Irene's story.

So, what was Irene's perception of her illness and other people's response? Denise decided she would encourage Irene to be blunt, reminding her this wasn't a doctor's surgery, time wasn't too limited, and her feelings were as important as facts. Slowly Irene told her story. She hated the well meaning, but nonetheless, slightly degrading way in which teacher colleagues tried to cosset her. Any chest problem or child health worry was shunted away from Irene, and considered to be too distressing. There was no recognition that she might want (however hesistantly) to share her expertise about asthma. She had once cherished the prospect of her condition burning out, and the doctor had once said this was possible. Now though the condition was a companion for life, and she was insightful enough to realise it became more dangerous as she grew older and her chest got tighter. 'It's like having a parasite on your back, a heavy kid piggy back all the time', she said with feeling. Denise Cooper agreed, having heard not dissimilar analogies from diabetics, epilepsy and rheumatoid arthritis sufferers.

Activity

In preparation for future lifestyle changes, Irene was then asked to say something more about how she saw exercise and her asthma. The points about school games were known to Denise, but she wanted to know more about Irene's recent years. To her relief, Irene explained that she had until the last few months maintained a programme of short walks, mainly to get her mother out and about. There had been the odd game of badminton in the school gym, but she felt hopelessly slow about the court, so she chose her opponents very carefully. She understood that the condition wouldn't always 'catch her out' if she played, and that the drugs, used prophylactically, would help. Nonetheless, it was a nagging doubt in the back of her mind – that here, in her place of work, her chest condition might let her down.

As Irene described her limited amounts of exercise, Denise watched her breathing very carefully. There was no residual breathlessness after several minutes of her recounting her experiences, so that was encouraging. Her colour in her hands and face was good, with no indication of central cyanosis or other signs of a developing chronic respiratory deficit. At this point Denise checked Irene's pulse and blood pressure, and was able to note that both were within acceptable limits for a woman of her age.

Having explored Irene's physical activity, Denise then enquired about mental stimulation. As a teacher, Irene would probably be dispensing a great deal of knowledge to others, but she wondered just how much stimulation Irene received. This seemed important to Denise as boredom could undermine efforts to improve health, and in any case, further education about her asthma might prove useful. Irene said that she continued to read a lot, but there were times when she 'slumped in front of the box' (television set). This appeared to tie in with the lack of friends, and Denise began to conclude that Irene's social and mental welfare was not only affected by asthma, but could also be the key to her coping with it better.

Pain

Apart from the frustration already referred to, Irene experienced no emotional pain. Physical pain during asthma attacks consisted of a considerable tightening of the chest, which made her feel panicky, until she could self-administer her drugs. It was clear that she feared this pain, and the sense that it might mean admission to hospital. There were very real times when Irene felt that her health was out of control.

NURSING DIAGNOSIS

Denise Cooper is keen to take stock of all that Irene has told her, so she arranges to come back and see her the following week. At that stage, she suggests, they might agree some mutual ideas on what can be done about her problems. In the meantime, Denise buys a little time to gather more details from Irene's GP, and to formulate a diagnosis of what her client's needs are. Describing these in terms of role is quite new to Denise, but she consoles herself that health service re-organisation has made the notion of nursing role much more critical, so getting to grips with 'role' is not a totally new endeavour. Moreover, she is experienced in reflecting on how best to help people, when to intervene and when not to, so her possible roles are very real to her. This enables her to make a useful start.

Irene has been challenged to adopt several new roles, all of which impinge on her health. Most visibly, following the death of her mother she is required to re-organise her life and establish new contacts, or else face loneliness. This socially active role is impeded by her misgivings about her asthma and how others might perceive both that and her self-medication. While Denise did not inspect the damp parts of her mother's home (which Irene still looks after while awaiting sale), it seems reasonable that going out and about will help limit her exposure to possible mould.

Irene is also being challenged to be more pro-active, assertive about her needs, *vis-à-vis* her teaching colleagues. She wants to spell out how she feels able to cope with work, but that she'd like to set clearer parameters on how her health will be discussed or seen. If she can achieve this, there is a prospect that she will increase her range of friends too.

Lastly, but by no means least, Irene still has some way to go regarding the monitoring and managing of her own health. She has not recently seen her GP or really considered her weight gain. She sounds a little diffident about some aspects of her treatment, and lacks confidence in it, at least regarding the taking of regular exercise. Denise feels sad that Irene appears to have been helped to understand the basics of the condition, without detail being added or the emotional impact addressed.

Summing this up, she believes that Irene has the potential to develop new roles and to become much more active and in control of her own health. The death of her mother has been appropriately grieved over, but she is relieved that she has now escaped the discomforts of her cancer. Irene seems ready to move on. To this end, Denise decides that she will offer to fulfil a couple of roles with Irene. First, she will act as an update teacher on her asthma problem. Second, she will advocate Irene's concerns to health professionals and suggest ways she can tackle her school-based, health concerns. Throughout, she will attempt to offer Irene positive appraisal of her efforts.

CARE PLANNING

Sitting down the following week with Irene, she was delighted to find that her patient had some useful further thoughts of her own. The earlier discussion had helped her to clarify her situation a great deal, and she wanted some advice from Denise, but then to get on with the project of building her life up again. Denise caught herself smiling at the thought that this must be 'role taking', but then promptly moved on to suggest the problematic areas that she saw Irene facing. Summarising them as making new friends and gaining confidence, sharing health care needs with teacher colleagues, and refining asthma and dietary control, Irene was able to concur that all were now necessary. The suggestion that she would be pleased to act as teacher, advocate and appraising friend sounded a bit artificial, even formal at first, but it was accepted by Irene very readily. This led to them agreeing a series of short-term goals and just one long-term aim to begin with. They agreed to note them down shorthand, in Denise's care records and in Irene's personal organiser. Irene joked that it was just like a shopping list, 'things to get and things to do!' (see care plan in Table 5.1).

CARE IN ACTION

From the outset, Denise emphasised just how an improvement in one role would benefit Irene in her others. After all, Irene could live asthma, rather than suffer it. It was better to take control of events. With that in mind their first goals were very much active ones and each was arranged toward Irene's long-term aim, to 'take charge of her life once more'. It was comparatively easy for Irene to glean literature from the Ramblers' Association and their local group secretary was pleased to reassure her by telephone that their members came with very mixed walking abilities. Walks were graded both by length and level of difficulty (for example gradient), so Denise was able to use this as an illustration of how an exercise programme could be gradually built up. She suggested an exploratory Sunday afternoon meet and agreed to chat about it the following day, when she saw Irene during her first review visit to the GP.

In order to prepare her for that exercise, Denise felt it important to offer Irene a few guidance points. Firstly, there was no current, conclusive evidence that her asthma was exercise induced. She might suffer no symptoms whatsoever. As it was now winter (albeit a mild one), she should therefore quite consciously monitor how she felt. Pollen counts were down, but she should anticipate cold air and this might prove problematic. Dressing warmly and completing modest warm-up exercise indoors before going out on her walk were common-sense start points. Ensuring that she had taken her drugs prior to going out may also reduce the risk of exercise induced asthma (Paul and Fafoglia, 1988, p 159). Confidence was important at this stage, and Denise emphasised that the walk was very modest, with company, in an area close to medical facilities. If she became at all breathless, or uncomfortable, she should stop, and self-administer her Salbutamol.

Table 5.1 *Irene Walker's community-based care plan (Riehl/modified)*

Challenges:

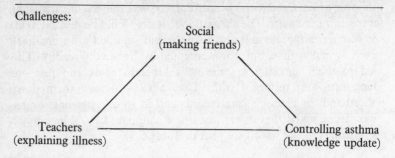

Social

Irene
1. Explore local Rambler Club membership
2. Invite friends to supper (share entertaining)

Denise
1. Teach Irene about exercise and asthma, control drugs and how to build exercise gradually
2. Review with Irene all that she has found out or learned (positive feedback)

Teachers

Irene
1. Itemise what I want teachers to understand
2. List what I fear about sharing these things with them

Denise
1. Assist Irene to plan what she wants to tell teachers and how this may be constructively presented
2. Facilitate an in-service training session for teachers on asthma (liaise with school nurse and Irene)

Controlling asthma

Irene
1. Summarise what I know about asthma
2. Review last few months – when did I become wheezy?
3. Keep diary during the next months, noting any illness or possible trigger factors
4. Visit GP and review my treatment taking along some written questions agreed with Denise

Denise
1. Update teach Irene on:
   a. trigger factors
   b. controlling the environment
   c. drug effects and use
   d. diet and calorie control
   e. problem solving (what to do in an attack)

Irene completed her list of facts she wanted to share with the teachers quite quickly. She disliked itemising what she feared sharing, but this was overcome when Denise suggested she draw up a short list of dates when she'd suffered an attack. This would then be used to emphasise just how comparatively well she was, and could be used to explain to the others that they need not mollycoddle her. Facts she wished to share, then, included what asthma was, what it felt like to have an attack, and how drugs could stop or limit these. It was emphasised how the condition came and went, but that she might need a bit of constructive empathy when the pollen counts were at their highest. Denise noted how she avoided mention of the inhalers, so she offered to explain how these worked using placebo—and to emphasise to the audience that if Irene stopped to take her medication it did not follow that she was necessarily suffering a bout of breathlessness there and then.

After some discussion, and consultation with the school headmaster, Irene, the school nurse and Denise booked a series of three lunchtime presentations on dealing with health and illness. These addressed the teachers' ignorance of diabetes, the female menarche and asthma, a wide array of health issues encountered by them in school. Irene agreed to introduce the series, with a few points about how it felt to be embarrassed, to rely on drugs or others for help. This set the theme of empathy – knowing how to approach a need, as well as what the problem involved.

Irene's review of previous months' health proved to be very vague, and Denise suggested she keep a weekly health diary for the current school term. In it she could record progress with her exercise, diet and drugs, as well as note the incidence of asthma attacks. Starting from Irene's list of known facts about asthma, and utilising health education pamphlets, Denise then arranged the specifics of what she would teach Irene about her situation. The teaching centred upon balanced drug usage and health monitoring. It also covered points about a calorie controlled diet and how Irene might cope if she became wheezy while out exercising. Remembering some comments about her mother's damp house, Denise asked if she would like to complete a review tour of her own place. There may be further allergens that the pair of them could identify as they walked around the living quarters. Irene agreed, and reaching the bedroom, explained how she carefully vacuumed the bedding and mattress, so as to deal with dust and mites. When they reached the living room, both agreed that the living room suite covers, and the rugs around the room, would need equally thorough attention, if dust was to be kept at bay. Irene had recently started to use a white board and marker pens at school, in preference to the chalk board, so chalk dust was also now much reduced.

EVALUATION

Four months later, Denise Cooper took time to draw some in-depth conclusions on her work with Irene. It was the occasion of a study day on health promotion and the facilitators had encouraged her to evaluate critically her work with one client. Because contact with Irene had been sporadic during this period of time, she had not been able to formulate the most comprehensive on-going evaluation of her client's progress. Still, there were some notable milestones achieved, so she noted these down, excluding Irene's personal identifying details, in order to respect her privacy when the groups reconvened to compare notes. Irene had most certainly become a more flexible person, a woman able to cope, take decisions and act upon the health advice offered her by the nurse and GP. She had joined the local Ramblers' group and added two new friends to her circle as a result. Her walks tended still to be modest, and always of the 'easy' or 'moderate' grades, but she had proved to herself that any tightness in her chest could be successfully controlled using her drugs and inhalers. Paradoxically, she could now use these openly amongst fellow ramblers, but retired to the school sick bay, to use them there. Irene was able to talk openly about this contrast, and Denise felt that in time, she might feel happy to be more open with her immediate teacher colleagues at least.

The health promotion sessions, including Irene's contribution, had proved a measured success. While some teachers felt unable to 'soak up' many more health facts, or pupil support considerations, they did warmly welcome Irene's suggestions on how to approach problems. As a result, Irene felt she was respected in the staff room, and welcome to question assumptions that she had to be protected from strenuous activities or health debate.

The diary that she kept throughout the term was both detailed and explicit, so that Denise was well able to develop her teaching about diet and drugs in a logical fashion. Unfortunately, despite increased exercise, Irene had not lost many pounds in weight. She suspected that school meals and the sometimes generous sized portions of pub lunches during rambles, were counteracting the modest calorie controlled diet advice, and benefits of walking. She would re-examine this area with Irene, hoping to help her recognise the threats of obesity during senior years.

In the social domain then, Irene had started to establish a new support network. She looked visibly more cheerful, and the stresses of work looked a little less heavy on her shoulders. This had partially helped her to present her health care needs to colleagues at work, confident that she was not as disabled as she first thought. Against this, Denise's health education had achieved only a patchy success. Irene was much more confident about her drugs, contact with her GP and exercise. Dietary control and openness about inhalers were only partially achieved.

To the surprise of other study day group members, Denise went on to reflect on her own roles with this client. She noted down these points under the headings of teacher, advocate and appraising friend.

Teacher

'I explained all the aspects about inhalers, the different drugs and asthma effects on the lungs clearly. I was able to change my teaching sessions to reflect just what my patient didn't put on her list as known. We agreed, together, everything that we would do, and achieved quite a lot of it. The rapport didn't suffer as a result of me being the teacher this time'.

Advocate

'My briefing to this client and her GP helped a lot. They had a really useful consultation and she came away with lots more confidence about exercise. I was a bit less successful in the school because, frankly, I wasn't sure how far to go on behalf of my patient'.

Appraising friend

'I think this was the best bit of all. It took a lot of time to get her moving, socially and in terms of trusting the drugs and her own ability to cope. It was only possible because I listened to her fears first, applauded her victories (nearly forgot that) and helped her take stock when she hit a worry. How do you quantify this bit of nursing care?'

IRENE WATKINS – REVISION QUESTIONS AND EXERCISES

1. Irene Watkins' health was intimately linked to her social welfare. Success in building friendships was good for her morale and, indirectly, important for her physical health. To what extent do you believe community nurses should become involved in these welfare issues?

2. Nurse Cooper's roles, teacher, advocate and provider of positive appraisal, are probably familiar to you in your own practice setting. She felt the positive appraisal provided to Irene to be important for success. What examples of positive appraisal have you afforded patients?

3. Irene found the use of inhalers stigmatising – she disliked using them in public. Can you suggest what the inhaler symbolically represents? (Hint: You may wish to make analogies with walking or other aids, or you may wish to draw upon ideas of what 'inhaling' or 'sniffing' a drug might represent.)

4. Irene's care plan was very abbreviated compared with those presented in other chapters. This was partly because Nurse Cooper worked in the community and partly because she was still developing her grasp of the Riehl Interaction Model. To what extent do you expect a given model of care to dictate what your care plan records look like?

5. Asthma is often an acute on chronic condition, 'flaring up' in response to trigger factors such as allergens. This pattern of hidden, then sudden and florid, illness, is very difficult to deal with for patients, relatives and work colleagues alike. Summarise how you think it might have affected the other teachers' responses to Irene.

Exercises

There are a number of support groups, charitable or self-help organisations whose purpose it is to represent the needs of patients and relatives dealing with chronic health conditions. The way these bodies present their members' needs is often important for funding of research, provision of resources and public response to the individual in the street. Choose one or more of these organisations and gather together the logos or other insignia that are used to sum up the group's purpose. You might find these among newsletters, charitable appeal pamphlets, or adverts in magazines or newspapers. Cut them out, or reproduce them by photocopy, in order to illustrate them to nurse colleagues. Before you do that however, ask yourself these questions:

(a) What is it about the logo which clearly identifies the group and the needs they're concerned with?

(b) Are there any negative or confusing aspects of these symbols?

In group discussion, it would be useful to examine just how we do collectively represent people's needs – so as to promote clarity, dignity and respect. Do you think this helps to make sense of how Irene felt about her inhaler?

In this second exercise, you're invited to play a word association game with friends. Perhaps you've played such games for fun before. The words we put side by side, are our shorthand for how we see the world and people within it. It can be argued that we can only make sense of our world through language, the use of word symbols. To complete this exercise you will need the co-operation of one collea-gue. Explain that you would like her to respond to a list of words you will offer, with the very first words that come to mind. The response should be short, crisp and quick. Ask permission to audio tape your short session, so you can both discuss the results, using the replay facility afterwards.

The purpose of this exercise is to explore the hidden associations that we all have concerning disease labels. In discussion, we hope that you will examine these and consider whether the patient with a chronic condition labours under a disadvantage because of similar associations and assumptions, linked to words. Here's the word list:

Wheezing
Asthma
Chronic
Drugs
Epilepsy
Allergic
Diabetes Mellitus
Intrinsic
Extrinsic
Cancer

CHAPTER SIX

Ben Tindell: Beyond the hernia repair

Elderly patients occupy a substantial number of hospital beds, and may make a more or less erratic rehabilitation from some types of surgery or other treatment. This is especially true if the admission to hospital was an emergency, and the patient has had to come to terms with the new environment under less than optimum circumstances. Ben Tindell's experience comes under just this category. A 74 year old man, admitted from a residential home for retired civil servants, Ben underwent an emergency herniorraphy, to relive his strangulated inguinal hernia. Without that surgery he might have died – but it nevertheless posed a sudden and complicating challenge in his life. His recovery following the operation is the subject of this the fourth Riehl nursing care study within our book. It covers the physiological needs of an acutely ill, elderly, surgical patient, and enables us to examine the roles that the nurse plays in limiting the risk of further harm to patients, while assisting them to manage post operative pain. Through examination of this care study you should be able to review the roles that nurses adopt as they make detailed patient observations and then the part they play in a patient's early rehabilitation. We hope that you will discover that an emergency scenario, such as Ben's, challenges the nurse to adopt some roles quickly, instinctively, allowing others to emerge in a more considered way as Ben starts to recover.

REVIEW OF THE SITUATION

It was a little before 1 a.m. that Ben was admitted to the on take surgical ward, suffering from acute abdominal pain, retention of urine and a state of shock. He looked pale and clammy, and he was agitated, both as a result of the last hours' discomfort and the sudden admission to hospital. Briefly, the nurse handing Ben over reported that he had been suffering from a minor chest infection, which caused him to cough a great deal. That evening, a severe bout of coughing caused Ben's bowel to herniate into his left inguinal canal, and there it became trapped. He had previously been diagnosed as suffering from a reducible hernia, and had been fitted with a surgical truss, to reduce it when he was up and about during the daytime. For two years this had proven a partial but largely satisfactory solution; but now surgery would be necessary. In greeting Ben, the nurse noted several things very quickly. He was an obese, elderly gentleman who presented with a dry, non-productive cough. He was clutching his lower abdomen, complaining of moderate pain. An IV infusion of normal saline (0.9 per cent) was running through a cannula in Ben's left arm. His pulse was rapid and thready, and his cold clammy skin confirmed his shocked state.

The casualty officer had issued several treatment orders to accompany Ben to the ward, and these included that he should be prepared for surgery within the hour. His urine retention was to be relieved by catheterisation, and he was to have a nasogastric tube inserted to assist in the removal of gastric fluid, and reduce the risk of complications intra or post operatively. The IV infusion was to be maintained at its current rate, and it was confirmed that blood had been taken for grouping and cross match, in case Ben required a transfusion.

Ben's pre-operative care had to be prioritised to equip him as quickly as possible for theatre. This meant that the nurse had to limit her information-giving role, but act promptly as a problem solver and care giver. To this end, she quickly started to gather some basic data (Figure 6.1). She introduced herself and assured him that she would be caring for him until his hernia had been repaired. Gingerly, she helped him into bed and removed his clothes, replacing these with an operation gown. A patient ID band was made out and attached, and Ben's dentures and small collection of valuables was recorded and safely secured away. His catheter was attached to a free drainage bag and details of his infusion and urine recorded on a fluid balance sheet. As the nurse worked, she helped him to adopt a comfortable position, lying slightly to his right with his knees bent slightly up. The nasogastric tube was aspirated and this fluid charted also.

Because Ben was clearly distressed by the upheaval and by his discomfort, she limited her explanation of planned care and the details of surgery. She knew that his ability to comprehend and

Figure 6.1 *Essential base line data collection: Ben Tindell*

Respirations: 28/min, shallow and hesitant because of pain
Pulse: 70/min (thready)
Blood pressure: 140/100 mm Hg (? hypertensive background)
Temperature: 37.2°C (axilla)
Last meal: 6 p.m. (main evening meal)
Pain: Abdominal (lower – moderate)
Current treatment: Nil
Sensitivities: Nil known
Urinalysis: NAD on catheterisation, 1300 ml obtained
Previous illness/surgery: Last op, tonsillectomy in childhood
Illness: some hip pain on mobilising for long periods (? osteoarthrosis
   linked to old age and obesity)
Reported body weight: '15 stone' (95.2 kg).

---

memorise much of it would be hampered under the circumstances, so those items of most immediate significance were covered first. She explained the procedures she was carrying out and emphasised how they would help Ben. He agreed that the catheterisation had helped already. It was possibly the case that his urine retention was brought about by local inguinal inflammation and stress; Ben had no history of prostatic problems despite his age.

Premedication followed (Papaveretum 20 mg/Hyoscine Hydro-bromide 400 mg) and within the period it took to record Ben's second base line observations, the theatre nurse arrived to escort him to the anaesthetic suite. They took him down along the corridors, and as they went, his nurse was already anticipating the post-operative care he would need, and the roles that her day shift colleagues would play.

FANCAP ASSESSMENT

At 0730 hrs the following morning, Staff Nurse Helen Gower and her assistant, Mrs Blake, took report of Ben's night time ordeal. The night duty nurse recounted Ben's admission, brief history and short pre-operative care record. He had gone to theatre where a left herniorraphy had been performed, leaving a redivac drain *in situ*. The bowel had indeed been twisted and appeared ischaemic. Without surgery, gangrene would have set in with dire consequences. Ben had returned from theatre with an IV infusion of Dextran in progress. Four units of blood had been prepared for Ben in the laboratory, but none had so far been necessary. His breathing post-operatively had been a little laboured, but his ability to sustain a clear airway had not been in question. Because of his previous chest infection and the anaesthetic gases, he coughed and this caused some wound pain. The night duty nurse had been concerned about this, checking his dressing and base line observations quarter hourly and then half hourly for signs of haemorrhage.

During the night he had received one dose of Morphine sulphate 10 mg and Prochlorperazine mesylate (Stemetil) 12.5 mg which had successfully eased his discomfort. She said that there had been no discernible additional depressant effects upon his respiratory rate, depth or quality. Helen Gower took the details down and made a mental note to get the care plan and base line details on to computer as soon as possible. It was going to be a busy day and Ben's situation would require a thorough assessment, given his surgery, age and physical condition. Accompanied by Mrs Blake the health care assistant she moved into the ward, ready to make her first assessment of Ben as she met some of his first comfort and hygiene needs.

Aeration

Given Ben's recent history, Nurse Gower began her assessment with 'aeration' rather than 'fluids'. FANCAP as a neumonic is a guideline to practice, and she was very keen to prioritise her care, ensuring that Ben's safety was her first consideration. She found him in the semi-recumbent position, well supported by pillows, looking understandably tired, but not as pale or clammy as he had been previously reported. He breathed shallowly and a little noisily through his mouth which would soon need oral hygiene care she thought. He had a sputum pot by the side of his bed, and the nasogastric tube was neatly secured along the side of his cheek. Introducing herself and her assistant, she noted the anxiety on Ben's face when the urge to cough overtook him. There would be a need to expectorate following anaesthetic, but it was clearly painful and he would need to support his wound while he did so.

A glance over his night time observation chart revealed that his respiratory rate had now settled to 24 respirations per minute and that no purulent sputum had been expectorated. She enquired briefly how his breathing felt and he confirmed it was better, 'catching only when his tummy pain caught him out'. He had smoked cigarettes until he was 60, but since then cost had made the habit prohibitive, so now his chest was in better shape than it might have been.

Without wishing to test his stamina, or unnecessarily make him more dyspnoeic, Nurse Gower was keen to gather a few early ideas on how the events made him feel. To this end she used open-ended questions, offering Ben opportunities to describe as much as he could rather than reply with a perfunctory yes or no. 'Frankly' he said, 'I feel a fool. I should have got the damned thing sewn up years ago'. His hernia was repairable and he had been offered surgery, but had never liked to take up hospital time, when other people were more needy. As for the trip to hospital, that had been frightening. He had felt grumbling pain all evening and the home manager, Mrs Percy, had fretted until he had agreed to the GP visiting. It was this doctor's visit that led to the ambulance being summoned, and his rapid removal to the ward where he now lay.

For Nurse Gower the story sounded familiar, but none the less interesting. 'Not wanting to bother others' could be seen as a trait among many elderly patients and she reflected it might have been the result of previous patient–doctor roles. In the past, you paid for a GP visit and hospital care. Summoning medical help was not only expensive, but took up the valuable time of a 'busy professional man'. All in all, Ben was relieved that the surgery was over. The ward was warm, the people seemed kind, so he thought he'd 'get along alright, even if it did look a bit strange at first!'

Fluids

Benn's state of shock, his intravenous infusion and fluid loss (urinary catheter, nasogastric tube and wound drainage in particular) formed Nurse Gower's next line of enquiry. Her first reassurances and questions shared with her patient, she and Mrs Blake began Ben's early morning hygiene care. It was an opportunity to inspect his wound dressing, review his skin condition, check his 'tubes' and develop the conversation a little further. Providing the wash, they noted that his IV cannula was firmly in place and the regime was running as expected. The cannula caused Ben no discomfort, but it irritated him to have his arm tied up like that. Catheter drainage was similarly satisfactory, the urine appearing clear. There was no sign of a haematoma within the scrotal sac (sometimes associated with inguinal hernia, blood draining down through the inguinal canal) and the catheter was appropriately secured, so it did not drag on his urethra.

These considerations apart, it was readily apparent that Ben was still dehydrated following the loss of urine, and fluid during surgery.

As yet, his IV fluid replacement did not appear to have redressed the balance. When Mrs Blake washed his skin, Nurse Gower noticed the poor tissue turgor, and this combined with his obesity led her to conclude that Ben would need an early risk assessment for both pressure sores (Norton *et al.*, 1978; Waterlow, 1988; Morison, 1989), deep vein thrombosis, and opportunistic infections (Hargiss and Larson, 1981; Messner, 1985) affecting his catheter, chest and wound. As a first step she used a pressure sore risk assessment scale (see Figure 6.2) described by Williams (1991). On this score, Ben was assessed to be at a significant risk of pressure sore formation. His score of 20, plus a growing pain over his bottom and heels, led her to recheck his skin condition at all pressure points. There were obvious signs of redness and she noticed that Ben had been very reluctant to move around the bed, for fear of further abdominal pain.

Examining his legs there was no evidence of pain in his calf muscles, or the popliteal space behind his knees. As a precaution, she asked Mrs Blake to help her fit him with anti-embolitic stockings and explained the function of these to Ben, who was advised to move his legs frequently, and to avoid crossing them for long periods while he lay still in bed.

Pain

Ben was suffering moderate to occasionally severe episodes of pain during the early part of his first morning on the ward. This was combated by a further dose of Morphine 10 mg intramuscularly as a prn dose. Nurse Gower felt less than satisfied with the pain relief plans that had provisionally been arranged. She was very much aware that surgical patients frequently did not have their pain relieved and that this could often have important consequences if Ben was dissuaded from movement – deep breathing, coughing, and, eventually, mobilising as a result. In the hospital there had been a tendency for doctors to stick to tried and tested analgesics and protocols that reflected their perceptions of what x or y operation would generate in terms of pain. Nurses too tended to undermine adequate pain relief, by failing to complete a fully individualised assessment of the patient's pain and then to deliver adequate analgesia within the parameters prescribed by the surgeon or anaesthetist (Hunter, 1991).

Figure 6.2   *The Medley pressure sore risk scale (adapted – as cited in Williams, 1991)*

Activity – ambulation		*Nutritional status*	
Ambulant without assistance	0	Good (eats/drinks/NG feeds)	0
Ambulant with assistance	2	Fair (insufficient intake to	
Chairfast (longer than 12 hr)	4	maintain weight)	1
Bedfast (longer than 12 hr)	6	Poor (eats/drinks little)	2
Ben's score = 5		Very poor (unable or refuses	
		to eat; emaciated)	3
		Ben's score = 2 (Obese)	

Skin condition		*Incontinence – Bladder*	
Healthy (moist/clear)	0	None or catheterised	0
Rashes or abrasions	2	Occasional (less than 2 per	
Decreased turgor/advanced		24 hrs)	1
age/dry skin	4	Usually (more than 2 per	
Oedema and/or redness	6	24 hrs)	2
Pressure sore involved	6	Total (no control)	3
Ben's score = 6		**Ben's score = 0**	

Predisposing disease		*Incontinence – Bowel*	
No involvement	0	None	0
Chronic but stable	1	Occasional (formed stool)	1
Acute or chronic unstable	2	Usually (semi-formed stool)	2
Terminal or grave	3	Total (no control)	3
Ben's score = 0		**Ben's score = 0**	

Mobility – range of motion		*Pain*	
Full active range of motion	0	None	0
Moves with limited assistance	2	Mild	1
Moves only with assistance	4	Intermittent	2
Immoble	6	Severe	3
Ben's score = 4		**Ben's score = 3**	

Level of consciousness (to commands)

Alert	0
Lethargic/confused	1
Semi-comatose (absence of response to stimuli)	
Comatose (absence of response to stimuli)	3
Ben's score = 0	

Score guide: 0–9 low risk
10–19 medium risk
20–36 high risk

Ben's total score = 20

It was true that Ben had undergone an anaesthetic, was elderly and had suffered a respiratory infection recently. Nevertheless, the risks of respiratory depression, and other opiate complications (Balfour, 1989; Lloyd, 1990) had to be balanced against the need to ensure his comfort, and limit the complications of immobility. Short-term opiate use should prove less likely to engender a dependency. Ben's cough was non-productive and difficult for him – so a compromise had to be achieved. Sufficient regular analgesia would need to be administered to facilitate physiotherapy, without markedly increasing the risk of cough depression and constipation. There would be a need to combine both drug and non-invasive measures to assist Ben in coping with his discomfort (Spencer, 1989).

Pursuing this, Nurse Gower used a simple pain thermometer drawn on to an A4 size board which had been laminated (Hayward, 1980) (see Figure 6.3). This could then be completed by Ben, using an acetate marker pen to indicate his level of pain. On a scale of 1 to 5, Ben reported a score of 4 prior to the recent post-operative injection of analgesia, and 1 after an hour post-injection. In addition, to discover the level of pain she also inquired about its location, type and constancy. The questions would not only assure Ben of her genuine interest in his experiences but also assist her to form an accurate picture of the pain, its likely, perhaps multiple origins, and its impact upon Ben's already limited ability to cope (copee role) (Marks and Sacher, 1973). In Ben's case, pain originated in his lower abdomen (especially his operation site), his bottom and his scrotum. Nurse Gower confirmed that Ben had recently had his bowels open, and wasn't of late suffering from constipation. As no swelling or tenderness was apparent in his scrotal sac, this pain was later attributed to a tension put on his spermatic cord by the hernia contents and the associated local oedema and surgery. His description of the pain varied, but there was a distinct gnawing ache in his 'belly' and additional more searing pains when he coughed and moved. The pain in his buttocks was ascribed to 'sitting too long on it', by Ben himself.

Activity

Linking to her concerns about Ben's immobility, Nurse Gower began to explore the limits of her patient's bed movement. She was eager that he sit up, move about the bed, and later that day, sit out in a chair (subject to no complications and medical colleague agree-

Figure 6.3 *Modified pain scale*

Pain assessment tool

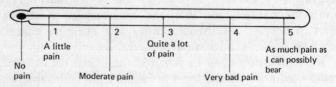

| | 1 | 2 | 3 | 4 | 5 |

A little
pain

Quite a lot
of pain

As much pain as
I can possibly
bear

No
pain

Moderate pain

Very bad pain

Using the marker pen, indicate your current level of pain on the
thermometer

Underline the terms that best describe it:

STABBING	DULL	INTERMITTENT	GETTING WORSE	FRIGHTENING
BURNING	SHARP	CRUSHING	GETTING EASIER	DISTRACTING
ACHING	CONSTANT	GNAWING	ANNOYING	PREDICTABLE
COLICKY	TWINGE	PULLING	GRINDING	SHARP

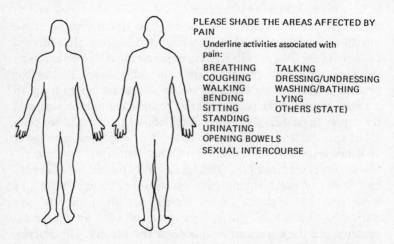

PLEASE SHADE THE AREAS AFFECTED BY
PAIN

Underline activities associated with
pain:

BREATHING   TALKING
COUGHING   DRESSING/UNDRESSING
WALKING   WASHING/BATHING
BENDING   LYING
SITTING   OTHERS (STATE)
STANDING
URINATING
OPENING BOWELS
SEXUAL INTERCOURSE

ment). Using a monkey pole or assistance from one of the nurses he
could move up or down the bed a short distance. Nonetheless, he
was both heavy to assist and clearly reluctant to move more than
extremely tentatively. She reminded herself that Ben would feel
tired and that rest was important to wound healing. Still, she
determined that it would be important to encourage him to do more
for himself during the later part of the day, and in those that
followed. Ben's apparent chatty conversational style made her realise
that he had a desire to please the nurses and to learn how he could
get better. He was, according to the residential home carers, a
normally active, enthusiastic man. His current immobility therefore

was probably the result of a mix of exhaustion and fear of pain if not actual pain itself.

Communication

During the first hours of Ben's morning on the ward, he had not received a detailed assessment of what his care was designed to do, nor had the nurses examined just what he understood about events. There was a balance to be struck, between rest, hygiene, safety and the need to understand his fears, anxieties and future expectations. Accordingly, it was in the afternoon, after he had captured a further hour's sleep, that Helen Gower explored this area with him. It emerged that Ben held a fairly passive idea of the patient's role – you did as you were told and didn't make a nuisance of yourself. The exception to this was reporting pain which he suffered with moderate stoicism. Ben registered a 3 on his pain scale and one of Nurse Gower's colleagues assessed this, before going to prepare a further dose of 'post op'.

They had expected Ben to feel disorientated, confused by the ward, but had been pleasantly surprised by his inquisitive nature. Assumptions about elderly patients were often open to question, and this seemed to be confirmed by Ben. He had no auditory or visual impairment that got in the way of a basic conversation. He was an intelligent man who interpreted his situation very functionally – his body had gone wrong, the doctors and nurses would help to put it right, much as a mechanic might tackle a breakdown. Whether this perception would help him accommodate later patient education was not quite so clear, but for now, he seemed reasonably assured about what was going on.

Nutrition

Ben was receiving no diet immediately post theatre, but his situation gradually progressed to hourly sips of water, and would later include soup and other light diet items. His considerable bulk was possibly going to prove both a strain on his wound site and a limitation to mobilising. Abdominal sutures and drains could encourage a patient to walk stooped forward and Ben's weight would not assist him to adopt a more upright posture. Nurse Gower established that Ben had been obese for at least a couple of decades, and that he was a snack eater, who supplemented his meals with digestive biscuits which he loved. He believed these to be good for his bowels, but readily admitted to being prone to the occasional bout of constipation too.

Within the rest home he had relatively few friends, being outnumbered by the women who had very different interests to him. Mrs Percy, the manager, however, was deemed to be a long-standing friend and she visited him that evening enquiring whether he had been comfortable since his operation. On balance, it seemed that Ben's lack of relatives (his wife had died ten years earlier, and they had no children) was at least partially offset by the well run and caring home led by Mrs Percy. He didn't particularly relish his return there later, seeing his admission as an adventure, but then again neither did he wish to get stuck on the ward.

Recalling Ben's dehydrated state, Nurse Gower checked his mouth and dentures, the next time she completed oral hygiene care. This consisted of providing Ben with a toothbrush, water, a receiver for his partial plates and encouragement to freshen up his mouth four times a day. His tongue looked less furred, his lips a little less dry. He admitted to being hungry, so it wouldn't be long before he commenced a fuller diet, especially as his bowel sounds had now also been confirmed.

NURSING DIAGNOSIS

Whilst Ben was very aware of his primary hernia problem and that this operation had been urgently necessary, he was less clear about the implications of immobility. Failure to mobilise now could delay his recovery. In order to move beyond being a passive recipient of care, Ben had several problems to overcome. Firstly, he had to receive a programme of pain relief care that would enable him to co-operate fully with his physiotherapy and general mobilisation. Secondly, the nurse had to assist him to see her as someone who reacted to his initiatives and needs as well as suggesting actions herself. His long-standing expectation that nurses cared for patients in bed would have to be confronted. Thirdly, and in the meantime, Ben would have to receive pressure relief, over his bony prominences and other pressure points.

A longer term initiative might then be directed towards Ben's nutritional state, his obesity and comparative lack of exercise. While he had no substantial health deficits beyond his current problem, and a mildly stiff hip, seclusion in a home where he numbered one other person as a real friend was not likely to add to his mental health.

Helen Gower discussed this appraisal with other members of the nursing team. It was easy enough to select some appropriate physical care measures from the menu offered by the computer care planning package, but she wanted to adopt a very active role in his rehabilitation. To this end she recognised she would start off as a problem solver (dealing with his pain and pressure relief), augment this as a care provider (sharing in hygiene and wound care, for instance) before concentrating upon a teaching role as she assisted him to mobilise. It was this last role which might seem new to Ben and which necessitated the establishment of trust between them beforehand. By helping to remove his pain, she felt this could be established.

Helen's care plan for Ben's first post-operative days was drawn from the computer menu and the printout of key goals was discussed with Ben. She ensured that he was left a copy of the document, their mutually agreed adjustment detailed in ink on both copies (see care plan in Table 6.1).

Care in action

During the following days, progress was evident in most aspects of Ben's care. The pressure risk assessment scale had been beneficial and the low air loss bed, assisted movement around the bed and early ambulation had combined to avoid pressure sore formation. On day 3 he had dropped into the modest risk category (score 9), as he was now mobilising to a limited degree, his collection of tubes had been removed and his nutritional status (high protein intake) was improving. The low air loss bed, while being a comparatively expensive piece of apparatus for a short stage of immobility, had more than fulfilled its purpose. It had protected Ben's pressure areas until such time as he became much more able to lift his body without discomfort. Nurse Gower reflected that it met most of the support system criteria suggested by research (Cochran, 1985; Zacharkow, 1985). Despite this, Ben's level of mobility was still rather disappointing, and this was largely due to the continued limited control of his pain. Collating Ben's pain experiences together, against the sporadic doses of post-operative analgesia and the limited level of patient independence, was proving a difficult business. It became clear that a number of variables, all of which could be adjudged to relieve discomfort, were complicating the picture of his continued pain. The removal of the tubes (including the wound drain) and the

Table 6.1 *Ben Tindell: post operative care plan*

Nursing diagnosis	Goal	Nursing interventions
Aeration problems		
1a Ben has undergone anaesthetic, is elderly and suffers from a chest infection	• Ben will be able to breath deeply and regularly 20–24 breaths/min. • Ben will cough/expectorate while supporting his wound to limit pain • Nosocomial chest infection risks will be limited	1. Deep breathing exercises hourly 2. Assisted to expectorate using sputum pot, pillow held over wound for support 3. Positioned in semi-recumbent or upright position (assist ventilation) 4. Resp. rate and depth monitored during each hour and recorded 4 hourly
Fluid problems		
2a Ben in a state of surgical shock	• Ben will re-establish a BP and pulse within his pre-trauma normal range (that is pulse 65–70 beats/min, BP 130/100 mm Hg.)	1. Maintain all base line observations 2 hourly during post op day 1, 4 hourly from evening day 1 onwards 2. Sustain IVI as per regime (see fluid chart) 3. Raise foot of bed to assist venous return 4. Administer increasing scale of oral fluids as per prescription 5. Monitor legs for signs of DVT (4 hourly)

2b Urinary catheter *in situ*

- Ben will sustain free drainage of urine
- Infection risks to urinary system will be minimised

1. Check catheter drainage 4 hourly (record on fluid balance chart)
2. Catheter bag emptied via tap
3. Catheter to be removed following medical review, monitor micturition thereafter
4. Catheter care daily (plain water and soap)
5. All drainage apparatus secured by bedside holders
6. Monitor body temp. 4 hourly for signs of nosocomal infection

2c Ben has a wound drain *in situ*

- Wound will heal normally, with fluid loss carefully monitored

1. Check dressings for signs of haemorrhage daily (do not disturb if nil evident)
2. Monitor blood/fluid loss via redivac drain and record on fluid balance chart
3. Secure dressing with non-allergic tape, note any local oedema or pain and report same to surgeon
4. Use aseptic techniques to limit opportunistic infection to wound

Pain

3a Ben's pain experience is inadequately monitored

- Ben will feel assured that we have mapped his pain experience fully
- Mapping of pain used to devise a pain relief protocol (discussed with doctors)

1. Explain rationale of strategy to Ben
2. Utilise pain thermometer chart 2 hourly (except when Ben is asleep)
3. Encourage Ben to bring his pain to our attention at other times
4. Chart all findings and analgesia provided in graphic form for discussion afterwards

87

Problem	Goal	Nursing Actions
3b Pressure area pain (bottom and right heel)	• Pressure will be relieved and all at risk areas regularly monitored	1. Monitor pressure areas 2 hourly while awake or providing hygiene care 2. Utilise low air loss bed 3. Move his position frequently 4. Sit Ben out of bed as soon as he is able (stamina, pain considerations)
3c Ben's pain irregularly controlled on PRN regime	• Ben will be assured adequate analgesia to meet comfort/rehab. needs. • Pain free state will be used as basis for physio and mobilisation programme	1. Pain control discussed with medical, physiotherapy and nursing colleagues 2. Ben assigned regular analgesia (as determined above) 3. Ben assisted with distraction therapy, deep breathing and relaxation exercises 4. Effects of pain relief measures monitored daily 5. Colleagues briefed on pain/rehabilitation symbiotic effects 6. Ben taught how to support wound when coughing 7. Review need for scrotal support when he mobilises
Activity problems		
4a Ben largely immobile in bed (risk of complications)	• Ben assisted to avoid risk of DVT, constipation, muscle wastage, foot drop and opportunistic infections	1. Assist Ben to use his 'monkey pole' 2. Maintain use of anti-embolitic stockings 3. Commence supported short walks (soon after pain-free state achieved) 4. Position 'tubes' so as to facilitate movement 5. Secure all tubes safely when patient at rest 6. Monitor base line obs. for complications 7. Reinforce the positive benefits of mobilisation to Ben 8. Support programme of deep breathing and leg exercises 9. Assist Ben with hygiene care until he is mobile

Communication problems

5a Ben has interpreted his role to be a passive one

● Ben will feel encouraged to take an active rehabilitation role

1. Discuss issues of informed consent and rehabilitation principles with Ben
2. Negotiate with Ben a programme of controlled exercise, bathing and deep breathing
3. Suggest ways in which distraction therapy may assist him to persevere with programme

Nutrition problems

6a Ben has been nil by mouth and has an NG tube *in situ* (free drainage)

● Ben will recommence a light diet
● NG tube removed asap
● Balance of nutrients will be chosen by Ben (calorie control longer term)

1. Monitor fluid loss via NG tube
2. Commence light diet, monitor what is consumed
3. Monitor bowel motions, assist with suppositories as indicated (Ben not to strain at stool)
4. Assist Ben with 4–6 hourly oral hygiene care (toothbrush approach)

6b Ben is obese and his weight might undermine his longer term health

● Ben will be able to review his dietary habits, weight *vis-à-vis* exercise, lifestyle and current problem (abdo. wound)
● He will be able to make an informed choice regarding his future diet

1. Weigh Ben every third day (progress monitor)
2. Review calorie intake, prospective future exercise, and discuss same with Ben and dietician
3. Discuss with him how excess body weight may increase health risks
4. Set out dietary options with a recommended plan for the future

89

reduction of his dressing size, certainly should have helped, but it was difficult to prove so, looking at his pain record. Ben reported pain in an erratic but challenging pattern, rising to scores of 3 and 4 on the thermometer five or six hours, then two hours, after some of his analgesia (Morphine 10 mg IM) injections. It was apparent that he feared his wound bursting open and having to return to theatre, so Nurse Gower had to acknowledge that psychological factors were undermining his response to physiotherapy.

What was more, she noticed a certain irritation in colleagues who tended Ben when she was off shift. The surgeons had written up three additional doses of post-operative analgesia but not (at least at her first attempt) agreed to a regular analgesia regime designed to run over the first 72 hours post operatively. While she was collecting details to advocate Ben's needs, some of the other staff seriously doubted that this patient needed that quantity of pain relief. They had reluctantly administered the doses of analgesia in response to pain chart readings and Ben's anxious expression. By the evening shift of post op day 2, Nurse Gower felt she must confront her colleagues in order to establish the role of analgesia in Ben's rehabilitation, and the nurse's role as an agent assisting the patient to feel control over pain, and to become a copee. The meeting turned out to be a heated one. The senior sister reminded Helen that the unit was not based on primary nursing, but a team approach, and her care planning with Ben had taken insufficient recognition of the experience of other nurses. There was, she insisted a very real risk of demotivating Ben through the drowsiness that could accompany doses of analgesia in an eldery patient's blood stream. Mobilisation required that Ben had an alert mind, and an excess of opiates could undermine this, just as much as it could remove the last vestiges of pain.

Helen Gower had to concur that a subtle balance had to be struck. Still, the progress of Ben was markedly less than they had expected, and even if he was compared with other elderly patients undergoing urgent herniorraphy (something she preferred to avoid), then he was slower by this measurement too. His shuffling gait and the nervous way he protected his wound site at every opportunity, did not tally with his otherwise bright and co-operative manner. She believed that he was still experiencing pain, felt he should minimise his complaints and that this in turn was slowing his progress.

While she had not consciously thought about it before, Helen now realised that role taking didn't just pertain to her relationships with Ben and Mrs Percy when she visited. It was a critical consideration, regarding the example she set with Mrs Blake and the professional relationship she built with the other nurses, doctors and paramedical staff of the ward. She was not sure that all her assessments were 100 per cent accurate, but she felt committed to advocate Ben's case to her colleagues and seniors. It was true, there were variables in Ben's progress she could not be an expert on. Nevertheless, his analgesia regime had remained prn, his progress was hampered by pain and Ben was slowly losing faith in the purpose of his pain chart. She challenged her colleagues to account for his hesitant mobilisation, to review the risks involved, and to question their own beliefs about Ben's apparently low level pain threshold and his likelihood of becoming addicted to his analgesia. After some debate, it was agreed that her documentary evidence should be set out in a joint surgeon and nurses' meeting. That was scheduled for the following morning.

As it happened, events were to develop that night which made Helen Gower's case much stronger. Ben began to show a pyrexia and it was discovered that he had either an exacerbation of his previous chest infection, or an opportunistic new one. What made matters worse was that there was also an ominous redness and mild oedema in his wound site. Coughing up small quantities of green purulent sputum, he did his best to support his wound, and apologised for getting stuck back in bed. He looked exhausted and anxious, as the doctors ordered micro culture and sensitivity tests on the sputum. A course of broad spectrum antibiotics was commenced, to be administered intramuscularly after a stat dose given via the intravenous route.

The following morning's meeting now became a clipped affair, Helen being invited to present the gist of her argument before the consultant's ward round. Weighing up the pros and cons, the consultant surgeon agreed that Ben's uncontrolled pain had been a major factor in delayed mobilisation and the resultant infection problems. He congratulated her on the reasoned approach that she had adopted and promised to speak to Ben about instigating a regular, oral analgesia regime immediately. In the meantime, a very careful monitoring of his chest condition would be necessary. Chest physiotherapy and deep breathing exercises would have to be encouraged, but these could be scheduled to occur approximately 1 hour after analgesia administration.

If Helen Gower felt vindicated as a result of the infection episode and the consultant's summary, she had little time to savour it. For the next 48 hours Ben became a very ill, elderly, almost frail looking figure. She turned her care plan priorities around once more, and now emphasised a problem-solving role rather than the teaching one which had been slowly emerging. Oral and body hygiene care, nutritional sip feeds, and the prevention of pressure sores, deep vein thrombosis, became the more prominent concerns. Assisting Ben to expectorate, to breath deeply and to gain adequate rest and sleep in the semi-recumbent position now filled her nursing shifts.

EVALUATION

Some 17 days later Ben was able to mobilise sufficiently well to be considered ready for discharge from hospital. During that time he had received a full course of antibiotics (Ampicillin 500 mg qds) and had undergone intensive physiotherapy to help clear his chest. Ben's wound was now neatly healed and the drain long gone. He reported that the experience had been 'decidedly rough' and that back at the residential home he was going to offer help in the garden, so as to keep active and fit. This was applauded provided that he commence his gardening duties no sooner than two weeks hence, and that during that time he consciously avoided heavy lifting, bending or stretching. Because of Ben's episode of post-operative infection, the opportunities to teach Ben about a modified, calorie controlled diet had been limited. Further, there had been only a limited time to help him plan an exercise programme. The nurses had concentrated upon the priorities, tackling the effects of his infection, the potential risks of relative immobility and maintaining a high standard of personal hygiene, especially while Ben was pyrexial. Nurse Gower talked with Mrs Percy quite generally about diet and obesity in the elderly. There was an agreement that many of the residents had a sweet tooth, and probably ate too much salt on their food, having experienced diminished taste sensation as they had grown older. Fibre was necessary, but it had to be presented attractively, so that it could form part of a satisfying, 'filling' meal and aid elimination (laxatives were a topic of considerable interest among the residents of the home). While she would need to discuss the idea of dietary change with all the residents, she was pleased to accept an opportunity to speak with the hospital dietician. At that meeting she would be able to gather a lot more additional details and take along a few previously prepared questions for investigation.

Turning to the issue of which roles Nurse Gower felt she should play with Ben and other elderly patients, there was a gradual consensual change of opinion that the analgesia problem should now be addressed head on. Both she, and the ward sister, in a later discussion, agreed that Ben's position needed advocating and that she had done this with integrity and enthusiasm. Any criticisms that the ward sister had held previously about the way Helen Gower communicated these concerns to others were muted by the infection events previously described. It was the case that nurses on the ward were unclear about their role in the prevention of hazards to patients – at least in complicated situations. All the nurses sought to minimise nosocomal infection, the incidence of deep vein thrombosis and pressure sores, but individual patient circumstances made care decision making not at all straightforward. Fears about the potent effects of opiates, the responsibilities concerning these drugs and the elderly, and the general background issue of drug-related litigation had all informed a comparatively defensive, conservative, nursing practice. If this was to be improved, standards of care specifically related to pain management would have to be much improved.

When Helen was asked to marshall her readings, the statistics she had collected concerning Ben's pain, together for a care standards meeting, involving both nurses, doctors and paramedical staff, she felt that her position had been even more responsible. Clarifying the ideas she had drawn from literature, research, and her observations with Ben and previous patients required a lot of reflection. Nevertheless, the interest levels among all the nurses was now high, and she ruefully reflected that any emergent, formal standards of care written and agreed would be as much Ben's as the nurses!

BEN TINDELL – REVISION QUESTIONS AND EXERCISE

1. The role of the elderly patients in hospital is very much affected by the institutional roles they may have played outside. Ben had come to hospital from a residential home for the elderly. What part do you think this may have played in the way in which he coped with his hospital stay?

2. Ben's story illustrates well that care planning cannot always be preceded by a neat or extensive assessment period. Care experience can be untidy, pragmatic and driven by the needs of the moment. At what point do you think Helen Gower started consciously to adopt key roles with Ben? On what did she base her newly recorded plan of nursing care?

3. The dilemma concerning post-operative analgesia and/or patient advocacy is one that you can expect to encounter in clinical

practice. Presumably, nobody would wish unnecessarily to deny a patients pain relief, or to expose them to risks associated with either analgesia or immobility. The prn approach to many post-surgery patient's care seems under strong attack. Why do you think this approach had developed as hospital policy in many places to date?

4. As an elderly man, Ben was perhaps increasingly facing restrictions in his life roles. Surgery temporarily restricted these even more, but the limitations of his ageing body and living circumstances played their part too. To what extent do you think Helen Gower was sensitive to this problem?

5. Helen Gower practised care in a team setting, and with a ward sister who on this occasion did not completely agree with Helen's definition of the problems to hand. Other formats of care delivery are possible, notably primary nursing. How do you think team nursing affected Helen Gower's efforts to adopt a progressive series of caring roles?

6. It could be argued that nurses working in general medical, surgical and high dependency care settings are so overwhelmed with the physical care needs of their patients, that opportunities to adopt, consciously, roles that assist patients in an holistic way are few. Reflecting on Ben's story, and your experience, to what extent is this true? What are the consequences for patients and nursing, if we do not reflect actively upon ourselves, our roles and communication as a tangible resource to care?

7. When Helen and her colleagues could not adopt a full teaching role with Ben (because of constraint of time), they facilitated the education of Mrs Percy, the residential home manager. Are there any ethical or etiquette difficulties inherent in this?

Exercise

In this chapter we would like to offer you one, in-depth exercise for consideration. We feel that it demands considerable reflection, both upon Ben's story and your own attitudes and beliefs concerning pain relief. In Figure 6.4, you will find a summary of Ben's pain over a 48 hr period immediately post-operation. You may find it helpful to add additional notes taken from the text of this chapter. Having clarified all the relevant data with a colleague, and checked up on the effects, side effects and contraindications of Ben's analgesia in a

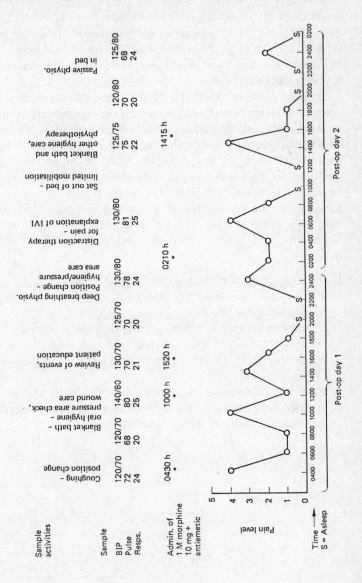

Figure 6.4 Summary of pain experience: 48 hours post op (Ben Tindell)

95

pharmacology textbook, in the library refresh your knowledge of herniorraphy, and the effects of ageing on drug absorption and excretion. Then, prepare to conduct your own informal series of interviews with qualified nurses and doctors. It is suggested that you explain this is a learning exercise, and that the patient details do not relate to a client of your hospital. Further, you should assure them that their views will be respected and their identity kept anonymous if that is what they wish.

Acquaint your interviewees with the circumstances of Ben's case (excluding Helen Gower's arguments concerning the effects of pain on Ben's mobilisation), and ask them to share their first observations on his pain record. We hope that they will identify that this pain is poorly controlled, so you can then move on to ask the critical question. So what should a nurse do about this? Having collected your convenience sample of data – discuss it with your colleague, noting down the key arguments. Prepare to feed it back within the discussion group which your tutor has organised. As you share that larger group discussion, bear in mind the following reflective questions:

1. To what extent was there a consensus of opinion on:
   a. Ben's pain (for example, thresholds, modes of expressing it)
   b. The analgesia regime
   c. Alternative approaches to tackling the pain problem.
2. What were the key factors which affected your respondents' position on this? (Did they mimic those adopted by some nurses in Ben's story?)
3. How will dilemmas such as Ben's be affected by the move to establish and improve 'standards of care' (as formal statements for quality assurance) within hospital?

CHAPTER SEVEN

Evette Lloyd and her bulimia problem

The image of a teenage girl suffering from an 'eating disorder' has become a fairly familiar stereotype both within the television soap opera and the popular social concern documentary. So effectively, in fact, that the profile of body image worries among parents and relatives has probably grown as a result – the spectre of anorexia haunting many families. Unfortunately this has also served to blur the definition of multifaceted problems, and it has done little to assist the patient who has experienced less chaotic weight control episodes, or who sustains a notionally normal body weight.

In this study we shall be exploring the needs of Evette – a 24 year old, young married woman who has Bulimia Nervosa and who is being supported by Gwen, her Community Psychiatric Nurse (CPN). It's a very apt situation for the Riehl Interaction Model, as both this condition and to some extent Anorexia Nervosa as well, are about symbolic actions and meanings. A slim body can signify youthful attractiveness, a diet represent control over not only body shape but life itself (Bruch, 1973; Palazzoli, 1974). Both conditions, and the challenges posed to sufferers, exist against a backdrop of cultural and fashionable norms of body shape, size and weight (Gross and Rosen, 1988; Nasser, 1988). These norms are negotiated within society, especially among the young adults of Western culture. How appropriate then, that a model founded upon the principles of symbolic interaction and socially workable, meaningful roles should be used by Gwen to assist both Evette and her husband Richard.

Reading Evette's story it will become apparent that Gwen takes a very conscious approach to setting up and modifying the roles she plays with this client. She is equally discerning about the Riehl model, judging that there is a need to add an additional, discrete body image care framework to complement the FANCAP assessment proposed by Riehl herself. Such on the spot clinical judgement is typical of Gwen and many of her colleagues. The view that all models must be in the service of care, and not dogma, is properly respected. This study does however show Riehl's flexible approach well to the fore, and emphasises strongly that nurses must be reflective and adaptable practitioners of care.

BULIMIA NERVOSA

Before turning to Evette's circumstances, it's useful to clarify what is meant by the term 'Bulimia Nervosa' as distinct from 'Anorexia Nervosa' (which some nurses may be much more familiar with). The *Diagnostic and Statistical Manual of Mental Disorders*, 3rd edn of the American Psychiatric Association (1987) summarises it as a condition displaying the following:

(i) Recurrent episodes of binge eating (large quantities of food being consumed in a very discrete period of time).

(ii) A feeling of lack of control over eating behaviour during such binges.

(iii) Regular use by patient of self-induced vomiting, use of laxatives or diuretics, strict dieting or fasting, or vigorous exercise to prevent weight gain.

(iv) A minimum average of two binge eating episodes a week for at least three months.

(v) Persistent over-concern with body shape and weight.

In contrast with the worst excesses of Anorexia Nervosa, many of these patients sustain a relatively unremarkable body weight – with an emphasis upon swings of behaviour rather than straightforward starvation weight loss (Rosen, 1990). This does not however exclude the pattern of some Anorexia Nervosa patients also employing bulimia style actions in their pursuit of an ever lower body weight.

Evette, like many other Bulimia sufferers, is an adult woman who has attained sexual maturity and, for long periods of time, has not attracted outsiders' interest. She is a private individual who has shielded her beliefs and habits, coming from a family background that would 'surely dissaprove'. While there is increasing agreement on what constitutes Bulimia Nervosa, less consensus of opinion has been achieved on how it should be managed. Different therapists emphasise different aspects of the client's problem, so Gwen's approach must be reviewed against this continuing debate. She uses an essentially cognitive behaviourist approach to Evette's problems

(Garner and Garfinkel, 1981). This addresses her perceptions and attitudes concerning food, eating and purging. She also draws upon a body image model that seems congruent with both this approach (her philosophy of care) and the Riehl interaction model (her way or organising her care roles). This model utilises a simple triangular representation of body image (Price 1990a, 1990b) and helps Gwen to explain to Evette what she is trying to help her achieve.

REVIEW OF THE SITUATION

Evette and Richard live within a small city flat, not too many miles from where they both work in the finance and business world. Both partners enjoyed a university education and anticipate secure careers in London. While Richard has always studied commerce, Evette originally debated a career in public relations and the marketing of high street store fashion. This was abandoned as the economic climate became more difficult, and her mother, in particular, warned against the precarious existence that could attend any fashion-orientated career. Since the age of 17 Evette has been trapped in a cycle of binge eating, desperate periods of remorse for her indulgence and a fear that the episodes would begin again. This led her to feel it was better to 'shade off' her weight by strict dieting. Her periods of guilt, almost depressive in their level of intensity, were accompanied by vomiting. At first, her university single study bedroom and toilet nearby enabled her to binge eat and then induce vomiting with her fingers pushed to the back of her throat. Finding the right calorific food (she preferred cheesecakes and gateaux) was difficult at night (when episodes were most common). Candidly, she confided that she had occasionally shoplifted frozen desserts, in order to hold a sufficient stock of food for the craving she knew would always come.

Marriage to Richard brought problems and rewards. While he strenuously began to encourage Evette to value her self and her studies, he was also close enough readily to witness the frequent binge eating and secretive, but nevertheless apparent vomiting of food that followed. Frequently, fervent conversations about fashion and her own 'saggy shape' were also a feature of their early married years. When he challenged her about the vomiting habit, the sudden bouts of cake eating, she was able to reply that 'lots of other women controlled their weight that way'. If it was erratic, and rather expensive, she was sorry, but she wouldn't tolerate a 'fat body' and her career couldn't benefit from it either.

It was an admission to hospital, for a right menisectomy (the long-standing result of hockey injuries while at school) that eventually brought Evette into contact with Gwen. In hospital, her repetitive references to food, her body's flabbiness, and requests for surgical removal of the 'dumpy bits' had finally caught the attention of a Staff Nurse. When Evette and Richard consented to see the hospital psychiatrist in order to explore this problem, she seemed relieved. Care in the community would be in the hands of her CPN, and the psychiatrist assured her he would monitor their progress, but Gwen was an excellent problem solver who could help them tackle the feelings and fears that she had.

FANCAP ASSESSMENT

From the outset, Gwen was concerned to establish a very adult and frank relationsip with both Evette and Richard. Her current degree studies had acquainted her with a great deal of sociology, and the discovery of a nursing care model based upon such theory intrigued her. Until now she had rarely stopped to reconsider the social aspects of her relationship with patients in quite such symbolic terms, so she was ready to examine the initial contact with Evette as both a nursing intervention and also as something symbolically negotiated.

To this end she wanted to establish Evette's perspective, not only on the bulimia habits, but whether this was seen as a problem, relatively normal or a completely pragmatic approach to weight control. She was also curious to understand how Evette viewed her as the professional helper, and the therapy she might offer. The fact that Evette had received a university education, worked within a business community and came from a middle class home might all be expected to affect the way she symbolically viewed the world and her situation in particular. It struck Gwen that forcibly or rapidly to challenge such definitions could place them in opposition to one another. She viewed it as her role then to glimpse Evette's perspective on things, without necessarily adopting this as correct, functional or healthy. All of that required tact, and this was a prime consideration as she started to visit Evette in her flat.

Fluids

Gwen's assessment of Evette was very concerned with her changes in mood and all of the trigger factors that seemed to be associated with her binging. Many bulimia sufferers tend to a pessimistic, even depressive outlook on life (Kaplan and Saddock, 1991), and it was evident that Evette experienced major feelings of self-disgust generally at her uncontrollable compulsions, her shape and the things it made her do. She reported that the awful compulsion to eat grew within minutes and she would interrupt business to rush off to a local delicatessen. There she would purchase ten or more slices of cheesecake, biscuits and pastries, carrying them off to 'stuff into herself', in the office rest rooms or a hidden corner. This made her feel panicky, the pressure building inside her abdomen so she was sure she would soon burst. That sensation was always the sequelae to the orgy of eating and she would relieve it by discharging the now hated, undigested food in a humilating rush to vomit down the toilet.

Occasionally these episodes took her out of action for an hour or more. She would return, drawn, tired, trembling – so colleagues guessed she'd been unwell. On most occasions however she had managed to limit it to much shorter periods, so her presentable image was once again put on show for all to see.

Gwen's gentle enquiries into the frequency of these changes, calmness to compulsion, binging to vomiting and back once more via a sense of shame and disgust, drew an honest reply. She had been doing it, two, three, four times a week, most weeks for several years. The cost alone in food, wasted food, had been significant, but there was no way in which she could resist the violent swings of behaviour. While alcohol consumption may not be a prominent feature in bulimic's experience, Gwen was keen to know about this too. Alcohol after all represented a possible, albeit apparent, control over feelings, perhaps blotting out the drive to eat. Against this, it could also represent a further loss of control, the very aspect of herself that she despised so strongly. The interview revealed that Evette drank very modestly indeed. There was no similar compulsion to abuse alcohol. On the contrary, she feared the loss of inhibitions, that she might under its influence indulge again in her binging.

Aeration

It was remarkable from the start that Evette talked calmly, openly about her problem, the disruptive effects it had increasingly brought to her life. She was articulate about the pattern of gorging and vomiting, and the expression of disgust was repeatedly made. When she was younger there had been times when she had hated her best school friend, a girl who was apparently grossly obese. She admitted

101

to a fascination in her friend's weight, the impact this had on her success or failure with boyfriends. When other teenagers had jeered at the companion, teasing her about her obesity, Evette had staunchly defended her. Still, privately, persistently, she had prayed that she would be spared such excesses of weight and all the humiliation that it brought.

Gwen noted the previous experiences of obesity and what this symbolically meant, but it wasn't yet a complete picture. She wished to establish just how Evette felt about herself on an average day. After all, she was well within normal weight limits for her height and frame size, but her picture of her body was perhaps not that simple. Evette was convinced that her body was ready to ambush her, gaining weight rapidly, at any moment. It was barely under her command, and tended always to be 'plump", especially during her menstrual period, when she felt especially unattractive. Remarking that pre-menstrual period women frequently retained extra body water, Gwen attempted to explore whether Evette could be more objective about her changing body state. The point was taken comfortably enough, but she felt that her plumpness was far more than that, extending well into the next cycle and often catapulting her toward another eating session.

Nutrition

The assessment of Evette's nutritional status involved Gwen not only mapping out her dietary habits, but also her actual and perceived nutritional needs. There was a real possibility that Evette could have very disordered ideas on how balanced her diet was, and how nutrients and other factors (such as work or exercise) related to body weight and shape. Moreover, Gwen's investigations also had to explore the sort of supportive or critical relationship she now had with Richard and had previously had with others.

Discussion slowly revealed that Evette was something of an expert on the calorie counts of most of the foods stored within the flat. She readily appreciated the calorie impact of pastries and reported strenuous efforts to sustain herself for long periods on a diet of salad and chicken in various formats. Effectively these contributed to her normal body weight (54 kg) but they also seemed to have a symbolic self-retribution role too. Evette celebrated the blandness of some of these meals, the plain fare of someone who couldn't be trusted with a sauce. Gwen hoped she would consent to keep a daily 'eating and feeling' diary. at least for the next couple of weeks, so when Evette agreed, she was able to affirm what a helpful first step this was (Hutchinson, 1982; Freedman, 1988).

Turning to her relationship with Richard, it was apparent that he was perplexed, but unreservedly in support of the way Evette was now tackling her habit. His perception of the problem was that bingeing and vomiting had become just that – her own neat, but very fickle way of beating down the body weight pounds. He had dismissed her points about body shape as being incidental, concentrating upon the obviously 'too radical' dieting techniques. For Richard, the issue of body shape (as he saw it, quite acceptable) and weight control seemed quite separate. When Gwen explained to him that they were not, he accepted that this was something he'd not considered carefully enough. Getting a handle on the links between them was now his way of thinking about the problem.

Communication

However briefly, Gwen felt it important to make a short assessment of Evette's physical capacity to communicate and reason. Extreme episodes of bingeing and vomiting could not only bring psychological trauma, but radical swings in acid–base and electrolyte balances – leading to possible disruption in thought and communication ability. There had been no emergency admissions to hospital for physical care, and Evette rarely got light headed, nauseous or strange, so she felt reassured by the summary. What was apparent as she talked, however, was the damage done to the enamel of her teeth. Her incisors were badly eroded and stained, owing to the repeated rush of stomach acid over them. Recently, Evette had begun to carry a toothbrush in her handbag, but she agreed that her teeth were in less than optimal state.

It was over two more meetings that Gwen painstakingly built up the picture of how Evette perceived her situation (Figure 7.1). This appeared to consist of a series of beliefs about body weight and preferred shape, her own self-will and the way others would value her. It also involved confusion on the issue of 'control' – the way she swung from excessive, severe dietary measures to florid bouts of eating with no control whatsoever. Gwen was by no means sure that Evette understood the concept of body image in a dispassionate way. For her it was intimately bound up with a low self-esteem, memories from childhood, and a driving need to succeed in her career and personal life.

Figure 7.1 *Evette's perspective of the situation (headings after Beck, 1976)*

---

1. *Personalisation*
   (Misunderstanding events, experiences in terms of self-reference)

   'My friend was fat and I'm guilty for not telling her how I felt'.
   'At work, they're going on about diets, recipes, hinting at what a slob I am'.
   'Richard loves the attractive thin women on television – he's reminding me how I fail'.

2. *Polarised thinking*
   (Misinterpreting situations in extremes such as nice and unpleasant, beautiful and ugly)

   'Being fat I'll never win promotion'.
   'Thin women are go ahead, in control – I rarely am'.
   'My colleagues are so beautiful, I'm just plain dumpy'.

3. *Arbitrary inference*
   (Jumping to conclusions without supportive evidence).

   'I couldn't make it in public relations work because I was too plain'.
   'My mother told me not to go in for it because she sees I'm like that'.

The more that Gwen reviewed the links between diet, control and body image and between Evette's feelings and Richard's and others' imagined perceptions of her weight and personal worth, the more Gwen concluded she needed a simple way of explaining key terms. To build a programme of education, behaviour modification, they would all need to be talking the same language.

Activity

Despite Evette's considerable attention to body weight, she did not involve herself in regular, planned exercise. The round of demanding work deadlines and an office lifestyle sapped her mental energy, leaving her tired and disinclined to arrange sporting activity. She explained that she knew she should exercise more, tell her superiors that she would take the time to put her life back in balance, but that goal never quite materialised as the portfolios built up. Gwen suggested that by not exercising in a planned way she had lost a control measure, a way of handling body weight without resorting to more drastic techniques. Indeed, calorific food would be a plus if she were to exercise regularly, fuelling her running or swimming at no cost to her body shape.

Pain

Evette had already described her distress at bingeing, the unsightliness of vomiting into the toilet. She expressed her fears about gaining weight, and what that might mean for her career. Even though she led an apparently normal life in others' eyes, it was apparent to Gwen now that Evette suffered significant unhappiness at her predicament. The fortuitous hospital contact had provided her with an opportunity to start putting things right – so now Gwen felt eager to start planning a programme that might help Evette control her compulsions, and feelings of revulsion or distaste, through a better understanding of her own body image.

NURSING DIAGNOSIS

Gwen could not pinpoint a single date on which she made a nursing diagnosis of Evette's problems. Instead, through the interviews, it grew piecemeal until such time as she felt intuitively it was time to suggest some more positive action, above and beyond just mapping the situation. She was aware that this was the role expected of her by both Evette and Richard – so she summarised her appraisal of the problems and shared these with her colleague, the psychiatrist, so as to brief him on progress and test out therapy ideas. It was clear that Evette was chronically failing to control many aspects of her life and that as a result she was using emergency, and very unhelpful, panic measures to try and regain a sense of control. The act of bingeing had elements of 'help – I can't cope', of 'comfort – I'm going to eat and I don't care what the rest of you value'; while the periodic strict diet was both a response to cultural norms concerning women's weight and figures and a test which she set herself, as a measure of self-worth. Both of these behaviours pivoted on the self-induced vomiting and utter sense of shame, which reminded her increasingly that the cycle of events controlled her life rather than her own willpower.

This was in many respects quite typical of a bulimic patient's dilemma; but what personalised it for Evette was her history of experience and feelings regarding obesity, her aspirations towards a high profile, body image conscious profession, and her relatively

105

newly developed role as a married woman. Even as they talked, Gwen thought that Evette was gaining the first real insights into the number of factors which affected her bulimic state. At this stage she had not been able to address just how they fitted together, nor what could be done to tackle them, but she did appreciate that she had to understand the network of events, beliefs, attitudes and fears if she was to recover a more balanced life.

Taking Riehl's perspective, Evette had very little role flexibility built into her life. She was not problem solving effectively, and was only recently starting to understand how the illness role (an apparently once functional way of dealing with body weight and feelings) was now becoming a strait-jacket from which she must escape. In a sense, Evette had taken some of the social expectations of the Western woman's role much too far. The cultural expectations of body shape, fashion, had been all too pervasive, and set unrealistically on a pedestal against other poorly developed factors which could enhance her self-esteem. At its most controversial, Gwen thought, Evette may even have been polluted by social norms, which challenge a woman to extreme self-introspection of her body image.

Putting all of this back in perspective required a mix of measures. There would need to be a process of education, concerning body weight and what was reasonably normal. She would need to learn about the impact of social pressures and to explore her feelings about what this meant for her, a young career-minded, married woman. Exploring her beliefs about 'normality', her past contact with obesity, the connection between body image and self-image, appearance and worth would also have to be integral to the programme. These exercises would necessarily have to include Richard at some point, as body image seemed to be an important aspect of their shared experience of marriage.

Alongside these discussions, and more obviously practical, was a need for some strategies which would help Evette to abort the bingeing sessions wherever possible, and put diet and weight control on a more rational footing. Gwen had already arranged for Evette to start compiling a daily diary – and through this she would be able to spot trigger factors for eating habits and discuss alternative approaches to tackling these. An exercise programme would also be helpful, as this was not only something that could alleviate stress at work, but the planning and running of it could assist Evette to gain further self-esteem.

What remained to be tackled was Evette's perceptions of what others thought about her appearance. The tendency to dress two sizes too large, to wear rather baggy tops or jumpers was a defence ploy that could only gradually be changed as Evette was supported through a series of 'projects', whereby she explored others' reactions to her dressing in more obviously shapely clothes. As Gwen reflected on this she concluded that the programme was designed to enhance Evette's role flexibility, through helping her to become a more proficient problem solver. Initially she would have to be helped to trust Gwen's own perspective of the problem, acting as a learner. Later, in proceeding through the exercise programme, the diary review and the 'projects', she would be encouraged to become a decision taker. Gwen realised that the triggers, cultural or otherwise, to bulimia would probably always remain *in situ*. It was their role to find ways of switching off a standard, and very unhelpful personal response.

Gwen's plan of action was almost a surprise to her. As she wrote it down it looked neither like a traditional care plan, nor the therapy notes she often set up with clients. Instead, it was time related, making first suggestions for their joint activity as Evette moved through the progressively more demanding roles. When she negotiated the programme with Evette, she would leave out reference to the possibly emotive role headings of 'copee' and 'decision taker', but the stages would always relate to these as she acted to teach, to illustrate coping and to liaise in decision making (Figure 7.2).

CARE IN ACTION

Gwen was confident that the exercises that she would propose to Evette had a sound basis in research and practice (Beck, 1976; Butters and Cash, 1987; Dworkin and Kerr, 1987). She was also happy that her relationship with Evette and Richard was adequately developed. What she was less sure about was how she would present the abstract concepts of body image and related needs to the couple. This was important as cognitive therapy depended upon a common mode of understanding, and this in turn was the key to deciding how quickly Evette was helped to move from learner role to, eventually, a decision-taking role.

A wealth of body image terminology was on offer, from psychotherapy, psychology and psychiatric sources, but these were often complex and based upon a sound basis in Freudian or other theory.

Figure 7.2   *Interaction plan: Evette*

Progress through all stages based upon mutual review of performance on stage notionally completed. (Rationale for interactions recorded in brackets but excluded as a record between Gwen and Evette. Instead, the rationale was verbally discussed.)

First stage: problem aware
I help Evette to map the problem, body image, behaviour, pressures, norms and social roles. I link the experience of her past to current roles in order to help her examine why she's not been able to avoid complusion eating.
(If Evette understands the complexity of the problems that led to her behaviour, she may not feel quite so self-depreciating. Respect between us may grow, a bond of trust based on not belittling the situation. She needs to establish an overview of the problem in order to understand the strands of therapy.)

Second stage: learner
Evette learns about culture and body image. We use the diary to explore these pressures and how that has felt. She is taught body image model (triangle: Price, 1990a, 1990b) as a way of describing these issues.
(Evette needs to achieve confidence in all the areas – an understanding of abstract ideas, if practical exercises later are to make sense.)
   She learns that 'perception' is not always reality. We negotiate this, and she has been negotiating on unsound premises. We identify trigger factors to bingeing and suggest distractions. Exercise is explained, both as a better way to maintain a healthy body weight, and to distract her from reliance upon extreme diet or vomiting post binge (the cycle which has trapped her). (If Evette understands that perception and negotiation of her roles and self-worth is within her grasp, then control of her life will seem possible rather than just attractive.)

Third stage: copee
We involve Richard more actively – asking him to reflect with us on the experience of Evette dieting and his reactions to her fears of obesity and unpleasant body shape. If this goes well, we prepare some mirror exercises, Richard and Evette discussing the good points about how she looks as they share a meal. (Evette fulfils a partnership role and Richard is a significant influence in her life. We use the trust they have built to form a new team approach to the problem, mutually affirming Evette's progress and resolve.)
   Weekly charting of body weight is now accompanied by Evette writing down positive statements about herself, her looks, chosen from her diary or made there on the spot. (The mirror and weighing scales are critical reminders of Evette's past 'failings'. They must now be

used to affirm her control and to facilitate discussion. Reminding Evette that perception can be distorted is the preamble to the next stage where more public 'projects' on body image are planned.)

Fourth stage – decision taker
Evette, with help, now plans a series of projects where she explores different presentations of her body image in public. At first these are closely supported by Richard (for example, a meal out). Then they will involve more explicit body image sensitive clothing in areas that are more challenging, such as a disco supported by husband/friend. (Eventually Evette has to test her new image, self-control and confidence on a wider stage. She has to understand that society is about performances but that these can be chosen, confidently managed as well as reacted to.)

Ultimately her projects will involve her adjusting her image alone, changing dress to work or going out with friends and colleagues (diminishing levels of support). Clothes will be graded as more figure conforming. In each project Evette will be assisted to anticipate other reactions to her and to accept and value the statements of positive regard that may come her way. She is assisted to anticipate the teasing, innocuous comments that may unsettle her and to rehearse ways of countering these. After each project a debrief occurs. (The projects are graded in terms of level of difficulty – so she is assisted to continue by the sense of success she may draw from the last. The pace of projects, and the size of steps taken, must be carefully monitored if the approach is to be constructive and clear.)

In the end, she chose to adapt the five concept terms that Price (1990a, 1990b) used in his model of body image. This was based on a triangular relationship between body reality (the body as it objectively is), the body ideal (the body as the individual would like it to be) and the body presentation (what Evette does with or to her body, in order to live comfortably in the social world). Gwen felt she could draw this diagram for Evette very easily, and substituting 'body as it is', 'body as you'd like to to be' and 'body as you arrange it or show it to others' made reasonable sense. In addition, the two remaining concepts, coping strategies (Bailey and Clarke, 1989) and social support networks (Cohen and Mackay, 1984), seemed especially helpful. In these concepts, coping could be seen as either 'direct', 'indirect'. or 'palliative'. A direct coping strategy was one that attacked the source of the problem, the stressor; while an indirect coping strategy was one that enhanced Evette's capacity to withstand the stressor. Palliative coping merely blotted out the worst excesses of the experience, and did not functionally help at all. In these terms, the vomiting and overstrict dietary control that Evette practised between binges were representative of palliative coping. They didn't address her feelings and fears about her body image. Helping Evette to become a copee and then a decision taker would involve Gwen redirecting her toward indirect and direct coping techniques (the exercises proposed within the programme).

Richard as her partner, and most significant support, would be important in reinforcing the message and substance of the exercises or projects. Evette would need positive self-esteem support, words of encouragement and a favourable comment on her efforts and results as compared with the past. Gwen felt it was her own role to offer a considerate and encouraging appraisal of Evette's efforts and, in due course, to help her build a sense of belonging among work and social colleagues.

It was a first success for Gwen when Evette so quickly understood the body image diagram and commented on how it summed up several aspects of the mess she was in. Over the next two meetings Gwen helped her to examine what she thought about her own body, and offered statistical comparisons of other women to highlight the difference between body as it really is and her own body as she would like it to be. Asking her to write down statements that applauded aspects of her body, Evette was able to draw up a list of hands, face, feet and neck, all of which were considered to be 'not too bad at all'. Spelling out the negatives concerning her stomach, thighs, hips and chest was then worked through, before Gwen asked her where she got the ideas from?

This was the beginning of a second detailed conversation in which Evette began to look at all the ways such opinions were formed over time. The influence of culture and fashion was illustrated by a review of the women's leisure magazines which rested on Evette's coffee table. It made Evette angry to realise a little more starkly that such influence over her idea of fashion could play a part in such unhappiness. While concurring that fashion was influential, even pervasive, Gwen did point out that it was often contradictory, transitory and affected by the values of all the different groups who made up society. Above and beyond the choice of being fashionable or unfashionable, Evette had the choice of adopting something or all of the different expressions of fashion. In reality, then, fashion was less 'big brother' than she thought. There was a challenge yes, but there were choices too.

Looking through her daily diary entries, Evette was struck by the number of observations that she had made about other 'fat' people. Fat people were getting a poor deal, feeling suspicious and struggling to get on in her office and the local community. Drawing several of the observations together, Gwen was able to encourage Evette to ask and partially answer several questions:

(i)   Are my guesses about how fat people feel accurate?
(ii) Do they tell me as much about the world out there as how I feel my body should look?
(iii) Am I building these views based upon memories – the experience of my friend at school?

Daunting though it first seemed, Evette began to conclude that her perceptions might not be accurate. While, objectively, obese people may receive less positive regard from others, this was open to other value systems and a degree of negotiation. There was too a chance, she decided, that her dislike of obesity was tinged with guilt feelings. While she had defended her friend at school she had been no better than the persecutors, feeling repulsed by excess body weight herself. Perhaps the driving concern with her own weight was more a need to avoid such criticism. Perhaps the stereotyped view of obesity was a way of avoiding a showdown with her own dislike of fatness. If you simply fought the flab, you might avoid addressing all the feelings it had once engendered within you. Upping the tempo of weight concern however, also set increasingly unrealistic criteria of what a nice, safe body weight could be. When even a marginal failure to reach that goal occurred, the disappointment could be devastating, triggering ever more stringent diets, gorging relapses and self-rebutting vomiting sessions.

It was becoming apparent to Evette that body presentation was not only about the baggy clothes that she wore, but the way she punished her body too. The control of her weight, her body as a whole, was all about presenting herself as the smart, efficient business woman. The lessons she had learnt about presenting herself at interviews or in meetings, could come to be more important than the professional expertise she offered, or the personality that made her unique and worth working with. As she put it, 'we're all obsessed with the wrapping rather than the present, aren't we?'

During the two months while Evette was learning about her problem, she felt compelled to binge on several occasions. Gwen had anticipated that this would be so, and together they identified several events which threatened to trigger it off. These included colleagues' inferred doubts about her ability (it was not objectively verifiable), irritable comments from Richard about her fussiness over what she

111

wore, and situations where obese women (but not so often men) were openly discussed as unattractive or lazy.

Gwen was reticent to move Evette too quickly into a copee stance, but she recognised that some degree of first aid advice, alongside education, was necessary. To this end she suggested that Evette play two ploys whenever a compulsion began to assail her. One, she would start a count to 10, forming a mental picture of flowing water, repeating to herself that a drink of water would be more refreshing. Two, should the trigger involve adverse criticism of other people's body weight, she would find the logical opposite or attenuated statement for each one levelled against the individual. So, for instance, 'she's fat and lazy' might become, 'she's well built and not that fast' or yet more positively, 'she's well built, but that's got nothing to do with her work!'

When these techniques were combined with the first discussions on the physiological effects of exercise, Evette reported that the compulsion to 'panic eat' was very much reduced. The idea of a swimming and badminton exercise programme appealed, both because it spelt a very practical control (allowing her to eat modified quantities of calories) and because it was an activity she could share with Richard.

As Gwen and Evette reached this point, they decided stage three had begun and that it was time to work much more closely with her husband. Evette was anxious to begin exercise, as the current modified diet already seemed a little unrealistic, so that an additional method of control in her hands would be welcome. Discussion with Richard proved to be a rather more hesitant process. Only slowly did he appreciate the importance of the lunches they all shared before the mirror, and the positive statements about how Evette looked. Against this, the twice weekly swimming session (early morning to avoid crowds at the pool) and once weekly badminton sessions did seem to be rather more 'of use' as he put it. While Richard could see the triangle model explaining Evette's problem, it was still a further leap to understand that the programme was moving her toward being an indirect and then a direct copee. His contributions of kind comments, desisting from impatience with her 'dietary fads', were relatively unstructured, but an undeniable help.

It was fully six months later that Gwen felt happy enough to suggest to Evette that she and Richard consider some stage four projects. As with so many community based, limited contact care, it was to be a compromise: seeking to preserve their forward momentum, without risking too much failure and through that a setback to the start. While the exercise programme, anti-compulsion ploys and body image education had gone extremely well (Evette's binges were down by 70 per cent) it was clear that stamina was flagging. The longer the programme extended, the harder it was for everyone's role to remain clear. The importance of their role functions (such as providing appraisal support) was beginning to get lost and there was a real risk that too much reliance would soon be made upon the exercise programme as Evette's central if not sole salvation. For this reason Gwen set up a meeting, and with the help of the psychiatrist suggested the body presentation projects. Introducing the psychiatrist colleague did not seem strange to Evette; she had met him on two previous occasions. His involvement now, though, was carefully handled, both to congratulate her on her progress to date and to add extra support to the idea that the proposed projects would help. These would provide the last, carefully arranged steps which would afford her a great deal of independence, and the opportunity to conclude with just a monitoring support from Gwen.

Deciding upon the number of projects, and what should be attempted in each, took an hour over coffee. Evette seemed impatient to try bigger steps, more daring dress, as long as Richard or Gwen were present. Even now, her jumper and skirt were not the voluminous items she had habitually dressed in before. Despite this, caution was advised, as two goals were being planned at the same time. One was the increasing freedom for Evette to dress as she pleased. The other was a gradual reduction in her reliance upon Richard or Gwen as affirming social support. To that end, the first three projects were humble in terms of dress steps taken and fairly generous in terms of support offered.

During the next five weeks these were accomplished with a considerable degree of satisfaction. Perhaps fortuitously, there had been few external triggers to provoke Evette to binge and she was elated at how it felt to be out, to dress in slacks that allowed others to see her 'still slightly podgy thighs' but to feel much more free than she had ever anticipated. It was time to move on to an over-twenty-one night at the local disco, and Evette felt able to wear a knee length A line skirt in what she described as a 'fashionable suede'. The compromise was talked about carefully. Dress had to be suitable for this sort of setting, but she could not countenance anything that showed her thighs or her waistline too much. This skirt and a fuller jumper was the result, protecting the sensitive areas, while admitting that the contours of her hips and lower body could be exposed, at least under the subdued lighting of the club. In the event, she limited herself to drinking orange spritzers and watching the others dance. Debriefing the experience afterwards, Evette realised that she had not fully thought out what she might look like on a strobe-lit dance floor. She had felt secure in the half light and even warmed to the welcome shown to her by several colleagues who had also been there.

In contrast to the earlier projects, this had seemed a much bigger step forward. She felt she had made a significant gain, but of course, the venue had been filled with a large number of 'decidedly thin people'. 'Did you notice you emphasised the *decidedly* thin?', asked Gwen? Evette hadn't, but she smiled when Gwen pointed it out. There was confidence enough left for her slowly to tackle a few more projects and, yes, to discuss them afterwards.

EVALUATION

Evette's progress had been formatively evaluated at every stage of her programme, and Gwen felt that this was in keeping with the philosophy that she and the psychiatrist shared. It had been important to control the pace of the programme, and while a calculated risk had been taken, deciding to move on to stage four, it was agreed that it had been fully justified. Now, Evette was still involved in further projects, and was by no means secure enough in her body image to go for long periods without reinforcement. Still, she had a clear idea of her problems, was highly motivated to tackle them, and was building a month-by-month record which featured a reasonable diet, regular exercise and extremely rare episodes of modified bingeing. Even when Evette did give in to the compulsion, she was able to limit her session to four or five pastries, which would be 'burnt off' in a swimming session that was occasionally brought forward a day to compensate. Significantly, the sense of guilt was much reduced, and she reported no incidents of self-induced vomiting. While there was no means of corroborating this report, Evette did seem open and happy that she could share the temptations and limited 'failings' she had had.

Evette had established considerable insight into her predicament, and this seemed the most promising hope for a continued stable future. The means to reinforce the self-regard that went with this was a little less secure. While the social norms of thinness, her memories and self-doubts about others' perceptions could always trigger an 'eating panic' (to use Evette's words), there was less evidence to show that Richard or friends could or would consciously reinforce her confidence. Evette needed to have a little more freedom to eat over time, to diet and exercise in degree, and to feel in control enough to avoid the swinging excesses that characterise Bulimia Nervosa. Ethically it was debatable whether Gwen should even attempt to engineer that degree of support; so for the immediate future, she would have to limit herself to monitoring events – no matter how frustrating that might be.

EVETTE LLOYD – REVISION QUESTIONS AND EXCERCISES

1. In the exercise of psychiatric nursing care, the nurse uses herself very much as a resource, an integral part of therapy as well as someone who assesses and advises. Do you think Gwen's greater awareness of roles helped in this? If so, in what ways?

2. The programme of behaviour modification, and greater insight that Gwen and Evette negotiated, involved a number of stages. What decisions and dilemmas face the nurse as she guides a patient through these – the advancing roles of Riehl's Model?

3. Gwen's supportive role to Evette and Richard had its finite limits. Time, the pressure of other clients and commitments, an anxiety not to become over-involved perhaps. What are the limitations of such a major role with reference to education and associated care within the community?

4. In this care study an additional body image model is introduced, to assist the patient understand her problems. To what extent is it possible, wise or desirable to mix and match such approaches?

5. In the care study, Richard has difficulty fulfilling a completely supportive role to his wife. Given what you've read here, and understand about different family and gender-related roles, can you suggest why this may have been?

6. In some respects the most critical aspect of Gwen's programme was her move to help Evette confront the fact that her behaviour was not about body weight alone, but about how she dealt with her own body image. As you read the study, did you identify the trust that would be necessary for this to succeed? How did Gwen establish it with Evette and Richard?

7. Having explored the idea of a carer's roles, patient's roles and the role of the significant other (Richard – spouse), I wonder if you can now suggest what role or roles a nursing model has with regard to giving quality nursing care?

8. Gwen decides to interpret a lot of medical and nursing terms into more simplistic ones for use with her patient. Nurses frequently fulfil an interpreter's role. What do you think are the strengths and weaknesses, the benefits and risks of this?

9. The longer term success of Gwen's care remains still in the balance as we leave the story of Evette and Richard. Bulimia Nervosa sufferers may relapse and as we discovered, trigger factors cannot always be eradicated. Therefore, how does Gwen judge whether her care has been successful? Remember, as a Community Psychiatric Nurse she may be dealing with many clients whose progress is measured in very subtle ways.

Exercise

In this exercise we're going to explore the role of visual images, within magazine articles. You will recall that visual images symbolise (that is, distil or represent) a message. For instance, the dove represents peace; the lamp or the nurse's uniform, her caring role. Well now we are going to try and sensitise you to the ways in which pictures, images, create a message. This is important, for as you have heard, fashion images, a simple triangular model of body image, can both be significant in affecting how a patient thinks or behaves.

Using a popular magazine then, choose a picture (not an advertisement) that has been used to illustrate, encapsulate or enhance an article's message (don't read that at this stage!). Action pictures are best for this, though people's portraits are possible to interpret once you've practised. Look at the picture (artwork or photograph) and decide just what the key messages are. You might note whether these came to you loud and clear or whether they were much more subtle, even hidden at first. Write them down and then read the article to see what that adds. Having done this, ask a colleague to repeat this process with your visual image.

Once you have both done this, answer these questions in discussion:

(a) What symbols were being used to get the message across (they may have included words, on a sign or placard, for instance)?
(b) Did all the symbols work together to form one clear message for you? (If so, how? If not, what caused the confusion?)
(c) Now make the connection back to our care study. What sort of symbols were confused or misinterpreted by Evette and by Richard?

Having completed (a)–(c), we hope that you will see that our perception of the world, what is good or bad, acceptable or awful, healthy or unhealthy, is often relative and up for some degree of negotiation. Did you find yourself negotiating with your colleague over the meanings in the picture?

CHAPTER EIGHT

Carla Moore and the high dependency ward

Changing technology, a physically and emotionally demanding patient caseload, and the limited resources within modern health care services, all contribute to the stress that nurses experience. This is never more true than in intensive or high dependency care settings, or than among nurses who are making a significant role change. Under these circumstances the most precious resource of the health care system (its staff) comes under the sort of strain that can lead to the well documented, but perhaps poorly understood 'burn out' syndrome (Emener, 1982; Hancock, 1984; Bibbings, 1987). It's perhaps significant that in a caring profession, we have not always been that successful at caring for our colleagues. It is significant, too, that in this care study we return to a high dependency care setting, to describe the care afforded not to a patient (as in James Drew's story), but to a nurse, Carla Moore, who practices nursing within such a ward.

If Riehl's model is to meet wide ranging professional care needs, it should help us to explore the world of the carer as well as the patient. In this care study, a Continuing Education Tutor does just that, reconsidering a ward enviornment and the needs of a neophyte nurse, in order to assist in her orientation programme and minimise the considerable stress she experiences. Adopting a new caring role, Carla Moore has less time to review her own needs, but this is shown to be critical as she addresses the new environment demands. Only by understanding her own limitations, strengths and perspectives can she begin to become a successful copee.

Before examining Carla's story, however, let's review some of the key points made by the stress , coping and burnout literature as it applies to nurses in these sorts of settings. We cannot pretend that this will be an exhaustive survey, but it will help you to understand some of the knowledge base that John Evans (the tutor) used to tackle the experiences that Carla had.

STRESSORS, STRESS, COPING AND BURNOUT

Because John was assigned to facilitate the development of staff on the High Dependency Care Unit (HDUC: Longmynd Ward) he acquainted himself with the common stress problems that affect nurses and other staff there alike. Selye (1956) in a classic reference had long ago pointed out that a distinction should be made between stressors (factors which illicit a stress response in the individual) and stress (the experience of that interaction). What constituted a stressor was extremely personal, and depended upon the individuals' past experiences, their socialisation, culture and perception. Therefore stress is highly individualistic. That which stressed Carla might not stress other nurses working at the unit, for instance.

The stress experience can be seen to come into action when environmental or internal demands tax or exceed our adaptive responses (Lazarus, 1966). The extent to which this happens depends upon the individual's coping ability. Lazarus argues that coping consists of a problem-solving ability and the capacity to regulate our emotions. Moreover, the coping ability is determined by a perceptual process: deciding whether a situation is benign/ positive, stressful or irrelevant. Stress appraisal of whether the demand is harmful (it already had caused us hurt or damage) or threatening (it might cause us harm in the future) or challenging (it poses an exciting opportunity to develop) formed a secondary assessment of that which we encounter (Lazarus and Folkman, 1984).

From the previous chapter it's apparent that coping, too, is very individualistic. People have choices, and make choices, even though they rarely explore all of the courses available to them (Pearlin and Schooler, 1978; Bailey and Clarke, 1989). In many instances these are more or less successful. We 'get by', sometimes without too much recognition of just how that was achieved. When that *ad hoc* approach fails, when the stressors are too numerous, too complex, or our coping responses are too inflexible – then a state of burnout may emerge. Burnout is described as a syndrome, a collection of behaviours, symptoms and signs, that is characteristic of a maladaptive response to occupational stress (Jones, 1980; Cronin-Stubbs and Rooks, 1985). Figure 8.1 summarises the key characteristics of the problem, the state that possibly awaited Carla if she, her colleagues

Figure 8.1 *Possible burnout characteristics*

Presentation
Increased work but less productivity
Disengagement from the caring role (mechanistic methods of working)
Rigid methods of dealing with colleagues (distancing techniques)
Increased absenteeism
? Reliance/abuse of substances (such as alcohol)
Feeling of chronic fatigue
Reduced response to minor illnesses (slowed recovery)
Gastrointestinal disturbances
Weight change (marked gain or loss)
Disturbed patterns of sleep
Feelings of guilt or futility
Inability to make key decisions
Feeling disempowered
Repeated, salient, cynical attitude towards care and care goals
Feeling of boredom.

Contributing factors
Complex environment, poorly defined demands
Multiple demands – limited data on which to plan and care
Limited social support network
Unrealistic deadlines
Negative appraisal by others (poorly rationalised or explained)
Divergent, conflicting or poorly differentiated goals for the ward and
staff
Physically threatening or tiring environment
Repeated decisional stressors (for example, life and death decisions
without adequate debrief)
Under or poor staffing mix
Conflicting roles – either between professionals or roles assigned to
one professional
Presonality make-up *vis-à-vis* practice demands

Potential costs
Negative self-appraisal and even self-harm
Dependence upon drugs or other substances
Learned helplessness (why try?!)
Marital or other relationship stress
Lost income (absenteeism or dismissal)

Disrupted patient care
Poor quality patient care
Domino effect upon colleagues (especially junior)
Inadequate team or unit communication and resultant iatrogenesis
Loss of nurse from the profession
Financial costs to institution (for example, nurse replacement)
Disincentive to future candidates for recruitment (poor publicity for unit)

and John Evans were not successful in answering some of the HDCU issues.

It was John's experience that most nurses found the HDCU stressful, but for a wide range of reasons. The literature about stress and the Intensive Care Unit was mixed. While many studies highlighted the settings as more stressful than most, others were by no means conclusive. Death and dying (ever possible patient dilemmas on the HDCU) were significant (Bailey *et al.*, 1980; Hay and Oken, 1972) as were pressures associated with the pattern of work (Oskins, 1979; Nichols *et al.*, 1981; Campbell, 1985). Interprofessional relationships could also add stress for the nurse (Gray-Toft and Anderson, 1981) as could the demands posed by relatives (Cassem and Hackett, 1972). Against that, work done by Keane *et al.* (1985) suggested that ICUs at least, were not especially more stressful. Rather, it was possible (and John conceded this), that personality factors, job orientation, rather than the environment, could be the critical factor in stress and burnout patterns (Kobasa *et al.*, 1982; Ceslowitz, 1989; Kernoff-Mansfield *et al.*, 1989; Topf, 1989).

Practical experience of several HDCUs and the at times confusing literature had led John to conclude that at least three areas had to be considered in each stress problem. These were the environment, the individual (personality, skills and capacities) and the support system (professional or otherwise) that was afforded to or by the nurse. Each of these areas involved staff in key roles, and he quickly appreciated that role conflict or confusion could and did hold several of the solutions to dealing with the nursing staff's problems. Reading more about role, role models and role relationships, John was naturally drawn to the Riehl Interaction Model. While the nurses themselves might not have been familiar with the new terminology, he did think that it would enable him to study the problem (Figure 8.2) and to suggest a few tentative first solutions.

Longmynd ward consisted of 14 beds and supporting equipment, laid out on a modern ground floor building. As the HDCU for the hospital, it catered for a limited number of patients who had suffered coronary or respiratory life threatening episodes (6 beds) as well as patients who were recovering immediately after major abdominal surgery (6 beds). The remaining 2 beds were designated as a 'floating facility' and could be assigned to patients in either category or to patients admitted to hospital following trauma. Like many such wards, this unit was staffed by a limited number of qualified registered nurses, three of which were additionally qualified in the

Figure 8.2 *Stress and three different roles*

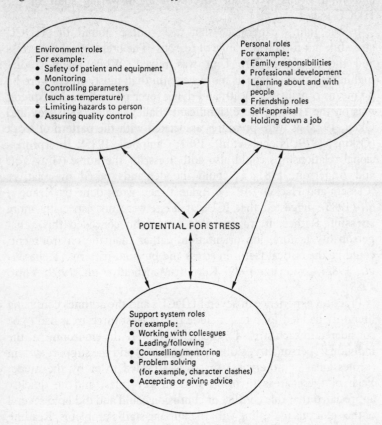

ICU or coronary care field. The bulk of the rest of the nursing staff was made up of nurses who were either awaiting specialist intensive care courses, bank or agency short-term replacements. Because of the above categories of patients, at least three different consultant 'firms' of doctors practise within the area, and this causes the RGN in charge (Sister Douglas) to insist upon a strict adherence to unit rules and protocols, 'lest the demands of so many others get us into a right mess'.

Carla falls into that group of nurses who have attained their registration, but who now seek a specialist qualification. She has staffed on a care of the elderly ward for the year post qualifying, and never encountered much intensive care nursing during her training – so she was very eager to immerse herself in this exciting environment. The rather more pedestrian pace of her last ward, however,

122

seemed a poor preparation for the demands and stringency that so obviously characterised Longmynd ward. It was as if the HDCU demands hardened the nurses, and sharpened the communication into a clipped, coldly functional harshness. At first, the precision of language, the technical expertise of the nurses had awed her. She was impressed by the efficient way in which the staff dealt with emergencies, and prepared for a whole gamut of eventualities that she could only begin to guess at. Then, though, she had begun to experience the confusion that often attended the clipped orders that came her way. She ran here and there, directed by the senior nurses – handling tasks so that quickly patients blurred together and she longed for the end of every shift. There had not been time to have a locally prepared induction programme, the unit always seemed too busy. It was as she had been fitted into a massive machine, and even though she was a spare part that fitted poorly, she would now be pressed into service. If she felt a cog in the machine, it was a cog that was getting more than a little worn down as she attempted gallantly to meet all demands, every shift.

John met Carla on his third visit to the unit. He had been recently assigned. He found her sitting in a small staffing room, staring out of the window, smoking what he was to discover was her fourth cigarette in succession. She barely appeared to notice him as he entered and offered to make her as well as himself a quick cup of coffee. It was very early morning and, outside, the ward was busy. Four patients were being managed post operation and three others were undergoing a battery of tests. The doctors who rushed about the place were young, anxious and irritable in their requests for equipment or laboratory results. Uncharacteristically, the second Sister in charge was showing signs of exasperation, wondering just where all the staff were. To enquire whether Carla was aware of the pandemonium outside seemed trite. John had been embroiled in one patient's care for 2 hours already. He had heard that another had unfortunately died that morning.

FANCAP ASSESSMENT

Fluids

Carla had now been working on the ward a little over 4 weeks. She was pleased to tell John about her first experiences, anxious to establish her reasonable approach to what the seniors asked of her, and delighted to have his calm interest in her concerns. The change from care of the elderly nursing had been considerable, involving not only a quickening of pace and increased technical work, but also a re-orientation of values. On her previous ward, success had been measured in different ways. If an elderly man was unable to mobilise completely, independent hygiene care and feeding could still be seen as a worthwhile achievement. The elderly woman who died, pain free, with relatives fully informed and adequately supported could also be a nursing success. Here, on Longmynd Ward, despite the general nursing philosophy of care being as important as cure, the stakes were often higher. The idea of salvaging a patient, combating systems failure, processing large amounts of laboratory and physiological measurement data seemed to take hold of nurses' souls. It was as if it were impossible to assign a wider range of goals than those already set by medical regimen. If the treatment failed, then implicitly, despite protestations to the contrary, the nurses felt they had failed too.

Momentarily, John felt compelled to ask her about the patient death that had occurred that morning. He suspected she would feel numb, and even cynical about how the nurses had dealt with it all. There was every chance that if he led her to such specific examples too soon, she would lose the thread of her lucid account. Instead, he asked about how each of her first 4 weeks had been on the ward so far. Carla was fairly clear that she had quickly become disillusioned with not only the values implied in some of the nursing care, but also her own ability to fathom how she might learn about intensive care nursing in this place. During her first week, it was as if her seniors could almost walk on water. There was a surety of manner, and the doctors so obviously respected the nurses' reports on the patients' conditions. The range of major problems and extended role skills that the nurses dealt with impressed her. Then, though, a mounting panic had set in. She felt increasingly less of an observer, and it was frequently the case that she was called upon to act without a very clear rationale. While she appreciated that emergencies often dictated this sort of request, it began to worry her that the next time around she wouldn't be able to respond adequately. It was as if each day a problem, a new admission or staff shortage, could ambush her, and it left her feeling extremely insecure.

At this point it was clear to John that Carla needed considerably more time to express her feelings and explore the needs which might help to explain what the ward was all about. A coffee break's worth of assessment was rather little, so he arranged to work alongside Carla for the rest of the morning shift. After that, during an hour or so before she had to get home to deal with her daughter's and husband's needs, he would have a chance to complete a more balanced assessment. Working with her, caring for a patient who had suffered chest injuries following a road traffic accident, John formulated the opinion that she was a skilled and organised carer. Her economy of movement, a quick witted approach, had been learned against a backdrop of many elderly patients waiting for her help. It was a skill, a capacity, that he was sure she was only vaguely aware of.

Aeration

The move to John's office proved useful. Not only was there now an opportunity to note down Carla's recent professional education, but there was time and privacy for her to air her feelings. She had moved to the High Dependency Care Unit in anticipation of post registration training in the field the following year. All the appropriate application forms had been submitted, and it had involved a lot of discussion with Andrew her husband. Learning HDC work involved sacrifices. Her work with the elderly had provided a substantial proportion of their income. Now, becoming a student again would force her into additional agency work and Andrew to extra child care duties at home. How did she feel right now? It was a little more difficult to say. Yes, she felt physically exhausted, but that was not unfamiliar to her. Past work had involved considerable physical care loads. What upset her more, though, was the feeling of being out of her depth, not in control of even the most basic care situations. She woke early in the morning worrying about the day ahead and, by late evening, she was still reviewing the care she felt she could have done so much better. It distressed her that the additional textbook reading, and the frequent circular worries she played in her head, left her absent-minded at home. Andrew and her five year old daughter Lisa could not be expected to understand the nuances of her new job, nor the size of some of the decisions she was often asked to make.

Listening to Carla's account of her feelings, John noted an implied criticism of the senior staff. He was aware that she had not received the usual 2 day induction package and had been thrown in at the deep end to help prop up the ward during an influenza epidemic. As a novice she sought guidelines, rules and regulations, explanations that would put a protective fence around those skills and that knowledge which she already had. There was a need to consolidate her sense of self-worth, to establish just how big her role could become. The fact that the experienced nurses of the unit had not apparently shared their insights could be due to many factors. Carla could only process so much new information at once, so information overload could have been a fear of theirs. Equally, many expert nurses are not aware of the subtle steps that they take in making smooth, efficient and timely care decisions. They could have been effectively dumb; unable to pass on in the most organised way the maxims, variables and considerations they took into account as they delivered expert care (Benner, 1984).

Carla's ability to verbalise her fear, her sense of exhaustion, impotence and doubt, was a helpful sign. She had until now lacked a dispassionate advisor to assist her in the process, and he realised that it would be helpful to act as her short-term preceptor as well as the planner of her education package. Aerating her feelings, with someone who understood the clinical demands, but who wasn't totally consumed by them, could be an important safety valve as she tackled the stress of her new post with all the roles that attended it.

Nutrition

John's appraisal of Carla's nurturant state was most concerned with her social support network. While she provided a degree of support to her patients, it was important too that she received support herself. Her role as a nurse, mother and wife was ideally a reciprocal one, in which she received rewards of love, help and advice from those that shared her life. Fulfilling multiple roles in her professional and personal life could increase the pressures on Carla, trapping her into double-bind situations, where to meet expectations of some would disappoint others. The extent to which Carla understood the compromises necessary within such multiple roles, and the amount of help she received, might determine her ability to cope with career change.

Carla's situation showed a sharp contrast between personal and professional settings. At home, Andrew was pleased to deal with a number of practical home and child care chores, and her mother assisted with regular periods of child minding. They had discussed the anticipated tiredness that she would surely feel, but there was only a limited understanding of what ICU work was like. Andrew and her mother had guessed there would be a catalogue of new conditions to learn, but the stress of decision making and taking had not been grasped. Despite this, Carla did receive a considerable

126

amount of praise and positive regard for her work and study efforts. It was a collective view that two skilled workers in the family was a safer employment bet, and promotion was always more likely the better qualified you were.

The contrast on Longmynd Ward was marked. Here there was expertise and a great deal of insight into the difficulties of establishing yourself. Sister Douglas acknowledged that all new nurses would feel very anxious about the monitors, the doctors, the patient's condition, and it had been these concerns that had guided the induction programme previously. What was currently missing was any particular nurse to whom Carla could relate. At first a ward mentor had been identified, but when this Staff Nurse went off sick, a replacement had not been nominated. As a result of that, Carla found that she took snippets of advice from anyone who could provide it. It was salutory, she reflected, that some of the most important geographical detail about the ward and its layout had been provided by a kindly ward domestic worker.

Communication

Following the work of the symbolic interactionists, John understood that Carla would need to negotiate her new role and that this was bound to be an ambiguous process. She was neither a qualified high dependency care nurse nor yet fully a student. She was newly qualified and presumably proficient in general care, but a complete neophyte when it came to special care procedures. She was not quite a member of the permanent staff, yet she was a regular carer, more experienced than many of the agency nurses. The way in which Carla would make sense of these contrasts was through agreeing parameters to her role. She would need to learn the informal norms of the ward as well as its formal protocols. Moreover, she would need to acquaint herself with the politics of the unit personnel's relationships. No job descriptions or brief could adequately map these or the symbolic behaviour of colleagues which would tell her all about it.

From the outset it was apparent that she didn't understand this process. She expressed hurt, irritation and even hostility at the half completed messages, and the way in which these could seem contradictory. At times she felt a pawn in a hidden power game – and reacted to the individual messages one by one, panic stricken. There had been few opportunities to examine what the messages collectively meant, or how these could be looked at to understand the dimensions of her new role. John encouraged her frankly to share her views and it was soon evident that Carla was able to observe other interpersonal battles, even if she was too raw, or too close, to understand her own communication problems. Two consultants vied with each other, to treat the ward as their personal territory. There were regular heated exchanges between them over the number of beds assigned to their patients' needs. Both valued the three qualified intensive care nurses and sought to monopolise these when it came to discussing patient care needs. This in turn seemed to have a negative effect on the other, non-specialist qualified staff nurses, who formed a second unofficial tier of staff. The consultants' behaviour, unwittingly or otherwise, drove (Carla thought) a wedge between the upper and the lower echelons of the nursing team. As a result the staff nurses began to squabble among themselves, greedy for their seniors' approval and yet eager to establish an experience-based credibility outside the upper echelon of nurses.

John asked whether Carla thought there were any other criteria of excellence, or success, other than the approval of the consultants? She had to admit that there did not seem to be. The nursing protocols, designed by Sister Douglas and a small working group, had come to be a professional defence mechanism, a way of dealing with conflicting medical demands. They had not formed a reference for quality nursing care, not did they seem to provide much leeway for practice; not that Carla felt equipped to nurse at that level yet anyway.

Because communication was so important in the HDCU arena, John took Carla's points seriously. He was already forming some disturbing conclusions based not only on her perceptions, but upon his own recent observations. The roles of doctors, nurses and paramedics on the ward should have been mutually complementary. Much of the work was problem solving, safety enhancing or involved reassurance-giving measures. This required a high degree of clarity in messages, and a cogent approach that would encourage patients, relatives and staff alike. At present, staff on the ward were not fulfilling their professional roles, because they were adopting behaviours more symbolic of parents and children. This meant that some staff behaviour was cynical, petulent and unconstructive, and was seemingly reinforced by the critical paternal attitudes of seniors, medical and nursing. Marriner (1979) has described the sort of assertive behaviour that would be necessary to put communication on a more functional footing. Following the work of the transactional analysis scholars (Berne, 1972; Jongeward, 1973) there would need to be an explicit recognition of the ego states being played out through some of the hidden staff roles of the ward. The destructive reliance upon parent–child relationships between senior and junior staff would have to be questioned, and a more appropriate balance established, using adult–adult and child–child relationships too (Figure 8.3).

Figure 8.3 *Transactional analysis ego states: caring models on Long-mynd Ward*

Parent ego state: (i) Nurturing (such as guiding, teaching, advising)
                          (ii) Critical (for example, should or should not rules)

Adult ego state: Unemotional, problem solving, practical state (goal setting and evaluating approach)

Child ego state: Dominated by emotions – rapid impulses, joy, delight, anger, hostility. It may be happy or destructive

Roles and ego states (possible examples)

Parent state: (Consultant/Senior Nurse – nurturing . . .)
Child state: (Neophyte nurse who needs time to attend to her feelings in a stressful new environment)
A crossed relationship, fulfilling role needs of leader and follower

Parent state: (Senior Nurse planning safety protocols . . .)
Parent state: (with other experienced staff in order to protect patients and inexperienced staff alike)
A complementary relationship, fulfilling role needs of the expert nurse

Adult state: (Doctors and nurses addressing care needs of a traumatised patient . . .)
Adult state: (involving relatives who can brief them about patient's medications at home)
A complementary relationship, filfilling role needs of professional problem solver and lay carer)

Child state: (Staff expressing relief at dignified and pain-free demise of a patient . . .)
Child state: (with relatives, who also need to feel it is normal to feel such relief)
A complementary relationship, sharing expressive roles

Activity

Building upon Carla's experiences, John then examined the forums for discussion and learning used within the ward. At present, four were in common use. These were: a series of consultant ward rounds, periodic paper rounds (when doctors and nurses reviewed case notes without visiting the patient), a weekly lunchtime clinical meeting (featuring medical led discussion of 'cases') and the nurses' shift handover reports. There appeared to be no explicitly inter-professional forums where staff needs were more directly met. The meetings were functional, patient centred and tended to minimise the importance of staff needs. Indeed, attendance at several of these led John to conclude that the ideal stereotype of a nurse was someone who was tough, technically competent, a good pacifier of patients or relatives, but who 'just got on with it' when stress was high. This apparent neglect of feelings, the attitudinal aspects of care, was familiar to him. High dependency care made huge demands upon nurses' knowledge bases. It demanded that they were skilful, both at traditional nursing skills and several extended roles agreed within the health authority. Because these areas were so tangible, obvious and measurable concerns when patients were so ill, it was easy to overlook the impact that such demands had upon each individual. It was only recently that the hospital appointments board had begun to look at the attitudes and qualities that would best equip a nurse to work within a given critical care setting.

Pain

Carla's distress in her new environment was apparent, and has been discussed already. Having accepted that, then, John extended his assessment of the situation. It was just as appropriate to assess the whole environment, the staff and their roles, if he was to afford Carla and her colleagues a useful amount of support. A visit to the personnel office of the hospital revealed several interesting facts. The unit had increasingly had to rely upon agency nursing staff, and the average length of stay for a non-specialist, qualified, 'permanent' nursing staff member was only a little over 10 months. When he enquired whether this was because they were filtering on to various post-registration courses, it was candidly admitted that this was only partially true. Seventy per cent of the Staff Nurses who had left during the last five years had left the specialty of nursing altogether. Two nurses had been apparently treated for 'nervous breakdowns' although this was hearsay evidence and difficult to verify. While the career moves of nurses was a very imprecise measure of staff satisfaction, John did conclude that it represented Longmynd Ward as an unhappy place to be. He believed, albeit tentatively, that there was such as thing as 'team pain', a collective dissatisfaction with work, clinical practice, which could undermine each of the staff's individual roles. The more he thought about it, the more he realised that clinical management, staff support and staff education could not be separated. The resolution of Carla's problem lay in the solutions that would have to be worked out collectively. To tackle her individual problem would be to tackle a symptom. To suggest staff education, before staff were reassured that their fears, hopes and aspirations had been recognised, would be to start out at too high a level.

NURSING DIAGNOSIS

It probably took John a month to draw together all of his conclusions about the problems facing Longmynd Ward. In the meantime he had started a series of twice weekly meetings with Carla, to reassure her about her work performance, to suggest the most accessible priority reading, and to let her vent her anger about some of the clinical dilemmas she encountered. This was his 'fire engine measure', designed to limit the risks of extra stress. In the meantime, though, his wider appraisal of the ward's needs was leading him to envisage a much more comprehensive plan of action.

First of all, he concluded that the staff were frequently not able to practise their roles flexibly and actively in response to the unique needs of their patients and daily changing situations. The fears of criticism 'from above' and litigation or censorship 'from without' were constraining the nurses in their decision-taking and problem-solving roles. What complicated that further, was the fact that the nurses were only indirectly aware of how the ego state games were getting in the way of them negotiating exciting responsibilities with their colleagues. It was as if they had developed, quite subconsciously, a formula for acting, and reacting, and that this, once useful, had now become a dogma which dictated how they should work with nurse or doctor. There had been no questioning of the hidden payoffs of such games, and the costs had, he believed, tended to accrue to the lowest staff levels, where nurses had voted with their feet, and left the unit.

Still at a very generic level, he began to question whether the balance of knowledge and skill based roles was fairly counterbalanced by expressive and attitude based needs. Nurses brought to their caring roles a battery of coping, a finite ability to soak up demands and when this was emptied, they either burned out or left. Always to meet the driving, professional needs of the patients and relatives, without reviewing the personal needs of staff, was false economy. The emphasis of case studies, medical or technological topics in unit meetings, reflected this imbalance. There was no evidence of counselling shared expression of feelings, as part of care or patient management. Perhaps it had seemed too painful, irrelevant or insubstantial. John was not sure which, but it seemed a critical need for the staff now!

Turning once again to Carla's account, John recalled all that he had read about reality shock. While at this stage, Carla was stressed, and suffering shock, he doubted whether she was burned out. Carla had experienced several stages quite characteristic of reality shock though (Schmalenberg and Kramer, 1979). First she had gone through a honeymoon period, when all that the staff said and did seemed expert and well founded. She had openly admitted to admiring the team, in a quite undiscerning way; blind to the petty competition that existed within it. The shock of discovering how such staff could then fail to recognise her needs, and overestimate her perceived abilities, had fallen upon her suddenly. She felt outraged that the personal ideal of high dependency care was tainted by pettiness, and an uncaring readiness to demand too much of new staff. She felt angry at her family, who seemed well meaning, but who also thought that her new role simply consisted of learning 'new conditions'.

To date, she had not evolved her own recovery methods. Perplexed, she felt she couldn't easily 'go native' and start to adopt the same cynical, defend your own corner style employed by other Staff Nurses. There was a delay until she could escape on to the High Dependency Care Unit course and, in the meantime, she had a wage to contribute to her family. This precluded her from job hopping, or simply quitting, which had more than once crossed her mind. Whatever resolution she came to, it seemed important to retain a human quality for her own and other nursing practices. It was perhaps not apparent to her at that stage, but high dependency care was not inherently impersonal. Nor need it be unsympathetic to the staff who are joining the care team. Rather, in John's estimation, Carla's reality shock was a problem of the clinical demands and the unhelpful way in which nurses and others responded to them on Longmynd Ward. For that reason, the bulk of his education programme would be personnel orientated. It would tread a fine line between teaching and counselling and between therapy and instruction. Whatever practical goals he would negotiate for the induction of nurses to the ward had to be based on attitudes and needs, as well as on skill and knowledge.

CARE IN ACTION

Because John was himself a comparative newcomer to the ward, and it would have been threatening to prescribe a series of solutions from outside the group – he decided to arrange a meeting at which he would introduce just a few first tentative ideas. Group work in any case was a gradual process, and while he might be able to itemise the problems and needs as he saw them, it was important for the nurses to feel their way into the help he could offer (Nichols and Jenkinson, 1991). As a result, the plan that John wrote was a guide to what he hoped for. It was not prescribed as the way forward to the rest of the group, and he fully expected to have to negotiate the roles that they would all play (Figure 8.4).

His first meeting became in fact two meetings. One, because he had been optimistic about the size of the agenda he could cover, and two, because several staff could not attend the first meeting. There was a sense of anticipation and the junior Staff Nurses in particular were keen to see what he would have to offer. When he openly admitted that he was not going to be offering a lecture series on care, there was some disbelief. It had been expected that his offerings would complement the doctors' talks and re-establish the status of local nursing. John though was quietly insistent. Until the environment had been looked at, as a caring environment, with multiple caring roles, there would be limited value in overlaying a series of superficial and possibly tiring lectures.

He was pleased when Carla backed him up, saying that she and others would benefit from this package of discussions and support groups – as these were as much education as the formal talks they had been used to receiving. If the staff was stable, and everyone could feel comfortable – learning together and not scoring points off one another – then the more conventional videos, lectures and seminars could be added later. As a result of that, it was agreed that three major projects would be put into action immediately. The junior staff job description and one for a mentor/preceptor were seen

Figure 8.4   *Longmynd Ward action plan*

Overall aims:
(i)   To enhance the nurse' role flexibility – by giving them the confidence to communicate clearly, assertively and with consideration
(ii) To establish a clearer definition of junior staff roles and the expectations that would be made of them
(iii) To encourage a balanced use of ego states as part of the interaction, the negotiation of staff and client roles
(iv) To facilitate an effective nurse/staff support on the ward (nurturing colleagues, assisting them to air their views and feelings)
(v)   To build an induction programme for new staff that takes into account the cognitive, skill and affective demands made within the unit

Enhancing role flexibility

(Fluids)
(a) Discuss with staff the importance of a stable team of carers, and examine how group morale might contribute to staff retention
(b) Encourage the team to build a series of short interviews by which a senior nurse monitors neophyte's feelings as she progresses through the first weeks on the ward (dealing with reality shock)

(Aeration/Communication)
(a) Establish a weekly meeting, for nurses, with coffee, in which I facilitate expression of problems and feelings
(b) In particular, re-examine the issues of:
  • Junior staff allocation
  • Ward jargon used
  • Assumptions of knowledge made by seniors on juniors
  • Common anxieties felt about expectations of seniors, by junior staff

(Activity)
(a) Following the work of Benner (1984), establish a series of workshops where the senior nurses do critical incident or vignette case studies to illustrate aspects of their decision making
(b) Reappraise with staff, their criteria for nursing excellence (*vis-à-vis* the protocols drawn up for the ward)

Clarifying junior staff roles

(Communication)
(a) Assist established staff to draw up a short list of the skills, qualities and performances expected of a Staff Nurse (non-specialist qualified)
(b) Discuss this, so as to formulate a new job description which is authentic to situation. Arrange for this to be ratified by hospital authority

(c) Monitor this document creation, and recommend clear requirements for ward preceptor and ward induction programme

(Fluids)
(a) Specify details of the ward work load, and the current ward philosophy, so that these may form up-to-date handouts to any new team member, even though their stay may be brief

(Activity)
(a) Suggest that junior staff roles should be highlighted at report handover. Encourage a novice as well as an expert summary of patient condition, so as to enhance potential for reflection and role development

Rebalancing ego stages

(Communication)
(a) Brief staff about transactional analysis, in order to introduce the function and features of parent, adult and child ego states

(Aeration)
(a) Assist them to explore how these states may have affected roles on the ward
(b) Encourage medical staff to attend, checking that all members of the group are reassured concerning group etiquette concerning such discussions

(Activity)
(a) Assist staff to value each of the ego states (role of staff works at each level)

Building a support system

(Communication)
(a) Suggest that a support group meets briefly bi-weekly, but more often in the face of clinical dilemmas
(b) Encourage ward team to view meeting this personal need as very professional

(Nutrition)
(a) Encourage everyone to map their personal support network (professional and lay)
(b) Suggest useful additions (introduce hospital occupational health leader and a counselling colleague – ? Phil to become a second group facilitator)
(c) Highlight the value of professional friends and where possible help staff to arrange gatherings of professional and lay helpers (social events)

(Activity)
(a) Post details of additional counselling or advice facilities locally, including my own educational counselling, on ward notice board

Building an induction programme

(Communication)
(a) Using a simple three column model (what they need to know, what they need to be able to do (skills), and how they may have to tackle feelings. Invite ward team to suggest key headings for future staff induction programmes

(Activity)
(a) Using above notes, prepare three day programme (6 half days) that emphasises a mix of active learning roles:
- Discussion (rehearsing fears and feelings)
- Guided self study (dealing with facts)
- Interviews (emphasising social skills and finding out about clinical/technical protocols)
- Critical incident analysis (emphasising reflective learning and facilitation by expert nurses)

---

as urgent necessities – so these were to be drawn up by the group of the senior nurses, led by John. The resultant suggestions would receive critical attention from the others as stage two of the process.

Project number two was the establishment of a small, voluntary support group. This would meet weekly in the coffee room and would have as its focus staff needs. Carla suggested that such a group shouldn't be purely a forum for gripes and grumbles but that it would be helpful for staff to bring along ideas of good practice, or useful antistress measures, that nurses had read about or experienced. It was into this embryonic group that John introduced the idea of expert senior nurses sharing periodic useful clinical experiences. These 'experience pictures' could illustrate the decision-making process and help the Staff Nurses to understand the dilemmas of decision making when situations went beyond what was covered in normal ward protocol. As John reviewed his suggestion, adding in reflective practice points, he felt it was a reasonable mix to suggest. In a very real sense, the unconscious coping strategies of seniors might add a lot to the discussion. The techniques proven in practice were often inadequately represented in any textbook of care or stress reduction.

The third initiative was very much a practical one. The nurses were universally keen to see a proper series of induction sessions planned for any other new nurse who came to join them. If they spelled out the key requirements, John could be getting on with building the programme and writing some of the material for them to check over and comment upon. John was pleased about this, and reminded them that his plan was to make the learning very active. There was little point in a protracted series of chats in his office, he reminded them. If the new nurse was to deal with the dilemmas, she had to explore feelings, as well as skills and knowledge.

EVALUATION

Over the period of the next few months, John began to formulate his evaluation of the action plan he had suggested to the staff. From the outset he was disappointed that they had not adopted any part of the measures designed to deal with the ego states which thwarted a more flexible plan of nursing care. This was (he suspected) because the criticisms went to the heart of the politics of the ward. To re-appraise the way in which Sister Douglas and others dealt with junior staff could seem an affront to their management. Moreover, it involved drawing the doctors much more into the group discussions, and this had only been achieved with one registrar who had previous support group experience when he had worked within an hospice. Whether he assigned the resistance shown to ego defences, a questioning of the implicit ward culture or something else, John was sure that the other measures would only partially control the stressors involved. In the discussion group, nurses repeatedly high-lighted that it was not just the life and death problems of patients that taxed them. That was periodically distressing, but what was more disturbing was the cloaked decision making and, at times, erratic manner in which leadership decisions were taken.

The longer the discussion group went on, the more this one item seemed to frustrate his efforts. Analysing the problem a little more closely, he concluded that it was in fact not all communications that proved a problem. Where procedures, protocols or patient progress were well anticipated and reasonably predictable, interaction tended to operate at an adult–adult level. Nurses and doctors worked together, problem solving and sharing plans with patients and relatives wherever possible. Where, however, the patient's hospital career was likely to be more uncertain, and the nurses role was therefore set against the diagnostic priorities of the consultant, senior staff behaviour tended toward a critical parent pattern. In the past, this had been tolerated but, now, several of the staff were slowly developing the confidence to share a lot of the ideas, worries and beliefs that guided their care. The irritable criticism of seniors was received with a calm, even a cool, and controlled interest. It was becoming rapidly clear that unless he drew all the staff into a wider, democratic discussion of their roles, fears about lost status could cause some of the staff to identify him not as a problem solver but as a problem maker.

Turning to the three projects set in motion by his first meeting, there was much more to be cheerful about. The working party that had considered the job description of junior staff nurses had excelled themselves. Not only had they drawn up a detailed and balanced list of responsibilities, but they had also added a second one for the nurse's preceptor. While the latter tended to feature a list of practical procedures and protocols which had to be inculcated into the junior, it did set aside a responsibility for enquiring about the nurse's own personal self-appraisal, before offering guidance comments on the progress to date. John had hoped that the preceptor's role would include discussing the ward philosophy with the student. As it stood, this document seemed to bear only marginal resemblance to some of the ward practices. On balance, there had been a clear progress. He had been able to ask Carla to test out the job description, and her first meetings with her new preceptor had so far been very helpful. What was more, showing the job description to Andrew and her mother, she was able to help them gather a fuller picture of the professional world she worked within.

The voluntary support group was perhaps the greatest of his successes to date, however. It met every Friday lunchtime for a little over 40 minutes and had successfully moved beyond the initial stage when moans were the norm. Two of the junior sisters led the group, and they had been instrumental in introducing a number of care discussions on roughly alternate group meetings. During these sessions they had examined patient stories and, in particular, the difficulties of dealing with relatives. Whether relatives were seen as fellow carers or other shock victims was a major topic of conversation. Spotting which way the relatives wanted to be treated was a key skill. If a nurse assumed that the relative was too upset to take a caring role, there was every chance that she would seem fussy, a 'know it all' who guarded the patient rather than guided him. If, on the other hand, she overestimated the relatives' readiness to help, then she might increase their anxiety several fold. What marked out the skilled nurse was her ability to spot the cues given off by relatives. It was this which might help determine the role that the nurse should adopt.

Above and beyond the practical illustrations of decision making, John noted with pleasure that the group had quickly set up a telephone network of home numbers. These were intended for problem solving when a nurse carried too much stress home with her. A code dictated that they were not to be used for calling someone back into work. Wherever possible, before ringing a colleague, the nurse was to note down several possible personal solutions, no matter how ludicrous they at first appeared. These then could form a practical basis for the telephone conversation.

Last, but not least, John had built an induction programme for new staff (nurses, and doctors, should they wish to use it), based upon the nurses' suggestions. The programme was founded upon six short projects through which a nurse not only explored the unit but also examined her own feelings as she embarked on a new area of practice. It started off with an interview with John himself. During this period, he showed them a video of the unit and this emphasised some of the typical monitoring and physical care measures that featured on Longmynd Ward. Discussion then followed, centred upon the ward's philosophy, and the beliefs and values of the nurse herself. The fact that she might not have verbalised these until now was not a problem. Clarifying personal values, and beliefs, was an important prerequisite to fulfilling a team member role. Other aspects of the programme featured self-study guides on intravenous infusion and fluid balance work, biohazards and infection control, legal aspects of care and sensory deprivation or overload. The interviews scheduled between the new nurse and the anaesthetist, the unit medical social worker and chaplain, and the senior sister, were all guided by briefs. These suggested to the staff ways in which the human aspects of patient care could be highlighted. John re-issued the briefs to staff everytime he made a new appointment for the newly arrived Staff Nurse.

The frequent visits to the ward, implementing this programme, afforded John opportunities to see how Carla had settled in. She reported that she was much happier and, indeed, proud of the ward and the way in which some staff so openly discussed their practice, feelings and coping strategies. There was now no doubt that she would go on to study intensive care nursing in London. When she went, she would take along the details of the support group meetings and especially the job description and staff induction programme.

'Don't worry', she assured him, 'if not everyone approves of what you're trying . . . it's made a big difference for me'.

CARLA MOORE – REVISION QUESTIONS AND EXERCISES

1. The study of Carla and the Longmynd Ward hints that staff on HDCUs may need to have special personality make-up to fulfil the role successfully. What qualities do you think would be important?

2. If the nurse doesn't have to have a particular personality trait (for instance, resilience), it may nevertheless be true that she will suffer reality shock upon joining the unit. Can you relate this to any personal role change that you have undergone? If so, what similarities would you wish to highlight?

3. It's apparent from this chapter that John is neither quite a full member of the Longmynd team, nor yet a complete stranger. To what extent does this help him to fulfil his role as an educator?

4. Figure 8.1 sets out the contributing factors and social costs associated with staff burnout. Carla had a responsibility to seek out help with stress and the staff to help her acclimatise in the least traumatic way possible. What roles and responsibilities do you believe the institution (the hospital or health authority as a whole) has to its staff?

5. To what extent does the staff and skill mix represented on the ward present a confusing picture for Carla as she seeks to establish her new role?

6. The FANCAP assessment has more traditionally been associated with patient assessment. Its role has been to help nurses organise their physical and psycho-social assessment of clients. To what extent does it help us to map Carla's role and associated stressors?

7. John, in his early assessment of Carla's emotions, desists from exploring her reactions to the patient death that so recently occurred. What are the pros and cons of this choice? Do you think that his role of educator has got in the way of being a caring colleague at this point?

8. John has to negotiate a workable role relationship with Carla. He decides that this requires more time than is possible in the coffee room, and a new environment away from the ward (his office). To what extent does time, and setting, affect the way you negotiate your roles with patients and colleagues?

9. The action plan which John prepared addresses the issue of ego states. As you will have read, his plan to rebalance these with staff never quite got off the ground. Moreover, the efforts have brought him into potential conflict with the consultants and one of the ward sisters.
   (a) Do you believe ego states constrain some of the roles nurses play?
   (b) If so, why are they used – what are their functions?
   (c) Given that John's programme could be undermined by belligerent senior staff – can you think of a strategy that might help overcome suspicion among them?

10. The account advocates, after the work of Benner (1984), that it is advantageous for expert senior nurses to share accounts of problem-solving care with junior colleagues. This is proposed instead of a conventional series of lectures from John Evans. What advantages and disadvantages might attend this expert nurse role alternative?

Exercises

In this the last exercise of this section, we'd like you to consider the issue of role change in a little more depth. It is, after all, recognised that significant role change (for instance, divorce or retirement) forms a major life stressor, and can fundamentally affect our health. We would therefore like you to conduct a series of three or four interviews, with colleagues or members of your social group, to try and establish just what they think this involves. You will need to ask the respondents their permission before proceeding and, of course, it's important to assure them of anonymity when you come to share your findings in discussion. To aid you in this, we suggest you use the headings overleaf. Setting them out on a large sheet of paper, it should be possible to record a good mix of useful data.

The aim of this exercise is to establish just what responsibilities or actions change as we go through role change. In addition, it is important to consider the dilemmas and questions involved, as the individual moves through the role transition. Once you have gathered your data, share this in group discussion and try to answer this generic question:

> What is the role of the health care worker as the individual goes through role change in life?

Here are the role change categories, and the suggested headings for you to explore. We hope that this, and all the other revision questions and exercises, have prompted you to think about the Riehl Model, and role-orientated nursing, much more generally.

Role changes

Worker to retired individual
Married woman to married mother
Employed person to unemployed person

First role (responsibilities/ behaviours)	Role change (key decisions, dilemmas) experiences	Second role (responsibilities/ behaviours)

Critique

CHAPTER NINE

A critique of the model

INTRODUCTION

The previous section has demonstrated how Riehl's Model of Care has been applied within a variety of health-care situations. The use of FANCAP as an assessment tool has been clearly demonstrated, and the development of in-depth assessment into therapeutic care planning, delivery and evaluation has been addressed through a selection of perspectives. The care plans have added considerably to the previously published British material (Arumugam, 1985, 1989; Aggleton and Chalmers, 1989), especially in the illustration of the working through of the plans. The care plans should be seen as 'developing the body of knowledge' in the application of a model that is still in its infancy. We hope that the text will enable you to consider using Riehl's Model of Care, or at the very least, exploring her theoretical framework and applying your new knowledge and skills appropriately.

AN OVERVIEW OF THE MODEL

Riehl's model is complex, and lacks definition, especially of its relation to practice. It has been minimally published, and there appear to be no evaluative or research-based studies.

The model was first introduced into the UK in 1980, being further developed in 1985 and again in 1989. It relies heavily on the theories of interactive communication, role and self-concept, and values the nursing assessment as the key to excellence in care planning. For nursing assessment, Riehl recommends FANCAP as the tool (Abbey, 1980). FANCAP cannot be used without interpretive understanding.

The model requires considerable background reading to interpret it. It is, therefore, not the model for the beginning practitioner. But, as the care studies (and Arumugam's earlier work) show, once interpreted and conceptualised, the model can be widely and successfully applied to deliver quality of care – care patients and families have a right to receive.

Key concepts

The source material for these has to be Riehl-Sisca's own publication (1989). Everything else which has been written is merely interpretative and applied. Her own work itself is scanty; the 1989 publication is primarily a summary of the work of others, while the care studies are British in origin (Arumugam, 1985, 1989; Aggleton and Chalmers, 1989).

Interactive communication

Riehl advocates the use of interactive communication in its widest and deepest perspective, using skills of verbal and non-verbal communication, and utilising it to make explicit what is implicit, thereby developing a comprehensive nursing history.

But, once the nursing assessment has been carried out, the model is weak on the other nursing skills – or at least appears to be weak from British nursing perspectives.

Little attention is paid in the source material to the two developing (or are they now developed) areas of British nursing intervention, namely the role of counsellor and the role of health education. Both roles are key – in both, the prevention of ill-health and the rehabilitation after illness are stressed. The care studies recognise this, especially the educative role. It is essential for patients to be given informed and correct information, and this is inherent in the Patient's Charter (HMSO, 1991). The teaching of relatives, and their need for supportive and therapeutic communication, is a key part of the care study on the young man with Hodgkin's Disease (Chapter 4).

One needs to ask whether or not the educative and counselling aspects of interactive communication are inherent within the model. I believe they are, but that future development of the model in practice must make them explicit, not implicit.

Self-concept

The understanding of self, as applied to both nurse and patient (and family), is also key to interpreting Riehl's Model for practice. These concepts have been developed within the care studies and will be better understood as nurses who are training under P2000 syllabuses (UKCC, 1986) complete their psycho-socially based studies and apply these to practice. The issue of self-concept of the nurse is widely explored in Jolley (1992). Nurses' self-concept is shaped by personal experiences, by their work environment, by their knowledge and by their socialisation. Their perception of care is important, as is their philosophy and expectations of the quality of care they should be delivering.

What Riehl does not discuss, and does not make explicit, is the stress that comes when nurses and patients develop therapeutic, supportive relationships. Campbell (1984) offers 'caring companionship' as one solution to becoming too stressed because it defines parameters for the relationship. Anyone using Riehl's Model must acknowledge this need for boundaries around relationships – anyone planning to use it would be well advised to read Wright (1990) and Ersser (1991) to explore how this stress problem is minimised within the primary nursing setting. This is perhaps even more important now that the Patient's Charter (HMSO, 1991) advocates the nurse:patient relationship developing through the 'named nurse'.

Role

Role is also explored in depth in Jolley (1992). It may be that role understanding and role analysis differ in concept in the UK from what is understood in the USA, but the various roles that both nurse and patient carry need further development. The care studies explore some of these, such as patient as student, conflict between adult and child, parent and son, but Riehl's Model would benefit from some examples from the theorist as to how she sees the model assisting role change and adaptation as the patient moves along the health–illness–health continuum. The role of the nurse as 'caring companion' (Campbell, 1984) and of the patient as 'partner' (Wright, 1990) may be unfamiliar to the American nurses, but is very real in Britain today. It is in these areas that the nursing profession in the UK has perhaps had most to contribute in the way of practice-based research.

Internal and external analysis

Stevens (1984) recognises internal and external criteria for evaluating models.

Internal criteria

clarity   – theory is understandable

adequacy   – the theory addresses all aspects of a model (the four core elements perhaps?)

logical
development – the model is systematic in structure

theory
development – is the model at the descriptive on analytical (explanatory) level?

consistency – are the terms and structures used with the model rational and symbolic?

Riehl-Sisca herself (1989) concludes that her model meets these criteria, and that 'it is at the explanatory level of development, in that it is being applied into practice'. From a UK perspective, one may not be able to draw the same conclusion. The reasons must be difference in education, attitude and perspective, but the clarity of the model is apparent only with considerable underlying psychological and communication theory input. Its adequacy as a model must also be questioned in that little is written on application to practice over and above the assessment – and the assessment itself draws heavily on FANCAP, rather than Riehl's Theory itself. The core elements are more than adequately defined and fit completely into the community care aspects of today's nursing role.

Once the theoretical framework is understood, the model is logical and stands at the analytical/explanatory stage – but needs many more published examples to ensure analysis is based on 'fair' content material. As is apparent from Section 2 of this book, those using the model (see also Arumugam, 1985, 1989; Aggleton and Chalmers, 1989) seem to have no problem with the consistency of the terms and structures.

External criteria

Stevens cites reality convergence, utility scope, complexity and discrimination as areas for external evaluation. Reality convergence applies to the Model's suitability for application in the care area of the present time – and of that there is no doubt since it addresses so many aspects of role and structure that have key importance today.

Therapeutic care, interactive communication and caring support are all keys to Riehl's Model and to care delivery in the 1990s.

Utility asks us to address its suitablity for application into the practice area. As a model, it has much to commend it; the weaknesses lie in the knowledge base which must be internalised before it can be applied, and in the shortfalls such as education and counselling which the user has to develop herself.

Scope addresses (rather obviously, one would think) the range of concept and application covered by the Model. Riehl sees the Model as exploring primarily biological and behavioural areas of knowledge and interpretation; I would expand this to suggest that its capability of analysis within the social field deserves recognition.

The Model is certainly complex in its origin, but in practice appears to be easier to apply than at first anticipated.

CONCLUSION

In Chapters 1 and 2 I said that the Riehl Model was not a model for the beginning practitioner. Analysis and evaluation confirm this. However, the skilled nurse who bases her care on a sound knowledge base and values clinical competency and patient/nurse partnership will find the challenge of application rewarding – rewarding both to her as a nurse and, perhaps more important, in the therapeutic benefits her patients experience through working together using it.

Chapters 1 and 2

Abbey, J. (1980) FANCAP: What is it? In Riehl, J. P. and Roy, C. (eds), *Conceptual Models for Nursing Practice*, 2nd edn, 1984. Norwalk, Connecticut: Appleton & Lange.

Aggleton, P. and Chalmers, H. (1989) Working with the Riehl Model of Nursing. In Riehl-Sisca, J. P., *Conceptual Models for Nursing Practice*, 3rd edn, 1989. Norwalk, Connecticut: Appleton & Lange.

Arumugam, U. (1985) Helping Harry to relate. In *Nursing Times*, 22 June, pp 43–45.

Arumugam, U. (1989) The Riehl model in practice with families and with staff. In Riehl-Sisca, J. P. (ed), *Conceptual Models for Nursing Practice*, 3rd edn, 1989. Norwalk, Connecticut: Appleton & Lange.

Benner, P. (1984) *From Novice to Expert*. Menlo Park, California: Addison-Wesley.

Bridge, W. and Macleod-Clark, J. (1981) *Communication in Nursing Care*. London: HM and M.

Campbell, A. (1984) *Moderated Love – a Philosophy of Professional Caring*. London: SPCK.

Ersser, S. (1991) *Primary Nursing in Perspective*. London: Scutari.

Gochnauer, A. J. H. and Miller, K. M. (1980) In Marriner, A. (ed), *Nursing Theorists and their Work*. St Louis, Missouri: Mosby.

Henderson, V. (1966) *The Nature of Nursing*. London: Macmillan.

HMSO (1991) *The Patient's Charter*. London: Her Majesty's Stationery Office.

King, I. M. (1991) *Towards a Theory for Nursing: General Concepts of Human Behaviour*. New York: Wiley.

Pearson, A. (1983) *The Clinical Nursing Unit*. London: Heinemann.

Riehl, J. P. and Roy, C. (eds) (1980) *Conceptual Models for Nursing Practice*, 2nd edn. Norwalk, Connecticut: Appleton & Lange.

Riehl-Sisca, J. P. (ed) (1989) *Conceptual Models for Nursing Practice*, 3rd edn. Norwalk, Connecticut: Appleton & Lange.

Simpson, H. (1991) *Peplau's Model in Action*. London: Macmillan.

Stevens, B. J. (1984) *Nursing Theory, Analysis, Application, Evaluation*, 2nd edn. Norwalk, Connecticut: Appleton & Lange.

UKCC (1986) *Project 2000: a New Preparation for Practice*. London: United Kingdom Central Council for Nursing, Midwifery and Health Visiting.

Walsh, M. (1991) *Models in Clinical Nursing*. London: Bailliere Tindall.

WPA (1990) *Annual Report 1990*. Western Provident Association Ltd, Bristol.

Wright, S. (1990a) *Building and Using a Model of Nursing*. London: Edward Arnold.

Wright, S. (1990b) *My Patient, My Nurse*. London: Scutari.

Chapter 3

Ayni, J. (1980) The severe burns. In *Advances in Psychosomatic Medicine*, **10**, 57–77.

Goffman, E. (1961) *Asylums*. Harmondsworth: Penguin.

Hunt, J. M. *et al.* (1977) Patients with protracted pain: a survey conducted at the London Hospital. In *Journal of Medical Ethics* **3**(2), 61–73.

Kubler Ross, E. (1970) *On Death and Dying*. London: Tavistock.

Muir, I., Barclay, T. and Settle, J. (1987) *Burns and their Treatment*, 3rd edn. London: Butterworth.

Parkes, C. M. (1975) *Bereavement: Studies of Grief in Adult Life*, 2nd edn. Harmondsworth: Penguin.

Patterson, R. (1987) Psychologic management of the burn patient. In *Top. Acute Care Trauma Rehabil.*, **1**(4), 25–39.

Price, B. (1990) *Body Image: Nursing Concepts and Care*. Hemel Hempstead: Prentice-Hall.

Raiman, J. (1986) Pain relief – a two way process. In *Nursing Times*, **82**(15), 24–28.

Riehl-Sisca, J. P. (ed) (1989) *Conceptual Models for Nursing Practice*, 3rd edn. Norwalk, Connecticut: Appleton & Lange.

Chapter 4

Baez, S., Dodd, M. and DiJuleo, J. (1991) Nursing management of persons treated for cure: Prototype – Hodgkin's Disease. In Baird, S., McCorkle, R. and Grant, M. (eds), *Cancer Nursing: a Comprehensive Textbook*, Chapter 43, pp 673–688. Philadelphia, Pennsylvania: Saunders.

Benner, P. and Wrubel, J. (1989) *The Primacy of Caring*. Menlo Park, California: Addison-Wesley.

Bonadonna, G. *et al.* (1988) Treatment strategies for Hodgkin's Disease. In *Semin. Hematol.*, **25** (Suppl. 2), 51.

Bramwell, I. (1989) Cancer nursing: a problem solving survey. In *Cancer Nursing*, **12**(6), 320–328.

Callery, P. and Smith, L. (1991) A study of role negotiation between nurses and the parents of hospitalized children. In *Journal of Advanced Nursing*, **16**, 772–781.

Carson, C. and Callaghan, M. (1991) Hematopoietic and immunologic cancers. In Baird, S., McCorkle, R. and Grant, M. (eds), *Cancer Nursing: a Comprehensive Textbook*, Chapter 35, p 552. Philadelphia, Pennsylvania: Saunders.

Erikson, H. (1980) *Identity and the Life Cycle: a Reissue*. New York: Norton.

Forbair, P., Hoppe, R., Bloom, J., Cox, R., Yarghese, A. and Spiegel, D. (1986) Psychological problems among survivors of Hodgkin's Disease. In *Journal of Clinical Oncology*, **4**, 805–814.

Grodecki, J. (1991) Malignant lymphoma. In Otto, S. (ed), *Oncology Nursing*, pp 200–214. London: Mosby.

Lazarus, R. and Folkman, S. (1984) *Stress, Appraisal and Coping*. New York: Springer.

MacDonald, M. (1988) Lymphomas. In Tschudin, V. (ed), *Nursing the Patient with Cancer*, Chapter 21, pp 341–354. London: Prentice-Hall (in association with the Oncology Nursing Society of the Royal College of Nursing).

McConnell, E. (1982) Burnout. In *The Nursing Profession – Coping Strategies, Causes and Costs*. St Louis, Missouri: Mosby.

Morse, J. (1991) Negotiating commitment and involvement in the nurse–patient relationship. In *Journal of Advanced Nursing*, **16**, 455–468.

Price, B. (1990) Normal body image. In *Body Image: Nursing Concepts and Care*, Chapter 1, pp 3–16. London: Prentice-Hall.

Riehl-Sisca, J. (1989) The Riehl Interaction Model: an update. In Riehl-Sisca, J. (ed), *Conceptual Models for Nursing Practice*, 3rd edn, Chapter 34, p 389. Norwalk, Connecticut: Appleton & Lange.

Chapter 5

Barnes, G. (1988) Asthma: latest developments in care. In *The Professional Nurse*, June, 364–368.

Brucia, J., Phipps, W. and Daly, B. (1987) Interventions for persons with problems of the lower airway. In Phipps, W., Long, B. and Woods, N. (eds), *Medical–Surgical Nursing: Concepts and Clinical Practice*, Chapter 48, pp 1360–1365. St Louis, Missouri: Mosby.

Cowley, S. (1991) A symbolic awareness context identified through a grounded theory study of health visiting. In *Journal of Advanced Nursing*, **16**, 648–656.

Kersten, L. (1989) *Comprehensive Respiratory Nursing: a Decision Making Approach*, pp 99–106. Philadelphia, Pennsylvania: Saunders.

Paul, G. and Fafoglia, B. (1988) *All About Asthma and How To Live With It*. New York: Sterling.

Richardson, H. (1991) The perceptions of Canadian young adults with asthma of their health teaching learning needs. In *Journal of Advanced Nursing*, **16**, 447–454.

Waterworth, S. and Luker, K. (1990) Reluctant collaborators: do patients want to be involved in decisions concerning care? In *Journal of Advanced Nursing*, **15**, 971–976.

Chapter 6

Balfour, S. (1989) Will I be in pain? Patients and nurses attitudes to pain after abdominal surgery. In *The Professional Nurse*, October, 28–33.

Cochran, G. (1985) Measurement of pressure and other environmental factors at the patient–cushion interface. In Lee, B. (ed), *Chronic Ulcers of the Skin*. New York: McGraw-Hill.

Hargiss, C. and Larson, E. (1981) Infection control, guidelines for prevention of hospital acquired infection. In *American Journal of Nursing*, **81**(12), 2175–2183.

Hayward, J. (1980) Can pain be measured? In *Nursing*, **1**(1), 32.

Hunter, D. (1991) Pain control: relief through teamwork. In *Nursing Times*, 24 April, **87**(17), 35–38.

Lloyd, G. (1990) Opioids in postoperative pain relief. In *The Professional Nurse*, August, 582–584.

Marks, R. and Sacher, E. (1973) Undertreatment of medical inpatients with narcotic analgesics. In *Annals of Internal Medicine*, **78**(2), 173–181.

Messner, R. L. (1985) Targets for infection: institutionalized elderly. In *Cancer Nursing*, **81**(8), 24–26.

Morison, M. J. (1989) Early assessment of pressure sore risk. In *The Professional Nurse*, **4**(9), 428–431.

Norton, D., McLaren, R. and Exton-Smith, A. N. (1978) *An Investigation into Geriatric Nursing Problems in Hospital*. Edinburgh: Churchill Livingstone.

Spencer, K. (1989) Postoperative pain: the alternatives to analgesia. In *The Professional Nurse*, July, 479–480.

Waterlow, J. (1989) Prevention is cheaper than cure. In *Nursing Times*, **1**(25), 69–70.

Williams, C. (1991) Comparing Norton and Medley. In *Nursing Times*, 4 September, **87**(36) 66–67.

Zacharkow, D. (1985) *Wheelchair Posture and Pressure Sores*. Springfield, Massachusetts: Charles C. Thomas.

Additional useful reading

Kick, E. (1989) Patient teaching for elders. In *Nursing Clinics of North America*, **24**(3), September, 681–686.

Lloyd, G. (1990) Opioids: routes of administration. In *The Professional Nurse*, September, 634–636.

Oberst, M. (1989) Perspectives on research in patient teaching. In *Nursing Clinics of North America*, **24**(3), September, 621–628.

Quilligen, S. (1990) When should you take your tablets? Teaching elderly people about their medication. In *The Professional Nurse*, September, 639–640.

Chapter 7

American Psychiatric Association (1987) *Diagnostic and Statistical Manual of Mental Disorders*, 3rd edn. Washington DC: APA.

Bailey, R. and Clarke, M. (1989) *Stress and Coping in Nursing*. London: Chapman and Hall.

Beck, A. T. (1976) *Cognitive Therapy and the Emotional Disorders*. New York: International Universities Press.

Bruch, H. (1973) *Eating Disorders: Obesity, Anorexia Nervosa and the Person Within*. New York: Basic Books.

Butters, J. and Cash, T. (1987) Cognitive–behavioural treatment of women's body image dissatisfaction. In *Journal of Consulting and Clinical Psychology*, **55**, 889–897.

Cohen, S. and Mackay, G. (1984) Interpersonal relationships as buffers of the impact of psychological stress on health. In Baum, A., Singer, J. and Taylor, S. (eds), *Handbook of Psychology and Health*. New Jersey: Erlbaum.

Dworkin, S. and Kerr, B. (1987) Comparison of interventions for women experiencing body image problems. In *Journal of Counselling Psychology*, **34**, 136–140.

Freedman, R (1988) *Bodylove*. New York: Harper and Row.

Garner, G. and Garfinkel, P. (1981) Body image in Anorexia Nervosa: measurement theory and clinical implications. In *Journal of Psychiatry in Medicine*, **11**, 263–284.

Gross, J. and Rosen, J. (1988) Bulimia in adolescents: prevalence and psychosocial correlates, In *International Journal of Eating Disorders*, **7**, 51–61.

Hutchinson, M. (1982) Transforming body image: your friend or foe? In *Women and Therapy*, **1**, 59–67.

Kaplan, H. and Saddock, B. (1991) *Synopsis of Psychiatry: Behavioural Sciences, Clinical Psychiatry*, pp 746–749. Baltimore, Maryland: Williams and Wilkins.

Nasser, M. (1988) Culture and weight consciousness. In *Journal of Psychosomatic Research*, **32**, 573–577.

Palazzoli, M. S. (1974) *Self Starvation*. London: Chaucer.

Price, B. (1990a) A model for body image care. In *Journal of Advanced Nursing*, **15**, 585–593.

Price, B. (1990b) *Body Image: Nursing Concepts and Care*. London: Prentice-Hall.

Rosen, J. (1990) Body image disturbances in eating disorders. In Cash, T. and Pruzinsky, T. (eds), *Body Images: Development, Deviance and Change*, Chapter 9, p 191. New York: The Guilford Press.

Chapter 8

Bailey, R. and Clarke, M. (1989) *Stress and Coping in Nursing*. London: Chapman and Hall.

Bailey, J., Steffen, S. and Grout, J. (1980) The stress audit: identifying stressors of ICU nursing. In *Journal of Nurse Education*, **19**(6), 15–25.

Benner, P. (1984) From novice to expert: excellence and power. In *Clinical Nursing Practice*. Menlo Park, California: Addison-Wesley.

Berne, E. (1972) *What Do You Say After You Say Hello?* New York: Bantam Books.

Bibbings, J. (1987) The stress of working in intensive care: a look at the research. In *Nursing*, **15**, 567–570.

Campbell, C. (1985) Stress survey: disturbing findings. In *Nursing Mirror*, 26 June, **160**(26), 16–19.

Cassem, N. and Hackett, T. (1972) Sources of tension for the CCU nurse. In *American Journal of Nursing*, **72** (8), 1426–1430.

Ceslowitz, S. (1989) Burnout and coping strategies among hospital staff nurses. In *Journal of Advanced Nursing*, **14**, 553–557.

Cronin-Stubbs, D. and Rooks, C. (1985) The stress, social support and burnout of critical care nurses: the results of research. In *Heart and Lung*, **14**(1), 31–39.

Emener, W. (1982) Professional burnout: rehabilitation's hidden handicap. In *Journal of Rehabilitation*, **45**(1), 55–58.

Gray-Toft, P. and Anderson, J. (1981) Stress among hospital nursing staff: its cause and effects. In *Social Science and Medicine*, **15A**, 639–647.

Hancock, C. (1984) How to beat burnout. In *Senior Nurse*, 21 November, **1**(34), 18–21.

Hay, D. and Oken, D. (1972) The psychological stresses of intensive care unit nursing. In *Psychosomatic Medicine*, **34**, 109–118.

Jones, J. (1980) The Staff Burnout Scale: a Validity Study. Paper presented at the Midwestern Psychological Association meeting, St Louis.

Jongeward, D. (1973) *Everybody Wins: Transactional Analysis Applied to Organisations*. Reading, Massachusetts: Addison-Wesley.

Keane, A., Ducette, J. and Adler, D. (1985) Stress in ICU and non ICU nurses. In *Nursing Research*, **34**(4), 231–236.

Kernoff-Mansfield, P., Yu, L., McCool, W., Vicary, J. and Packard, J. (1989) The job context index: a guide for improving the 'fit' between nurses and their work environment. In *Journal of Advanced Nursing*, **14**, 501–508.

Kobasa, S., Maddi, S. and Kahn, S. (1982) Hardiness and health – a prospective study. In *Journal of Personality and Social Psychology*, **1**, 168–177.

Lazarus, R. (1966) *Psychological Stress and the Coping Process*. New York: McGraw-Hill.

Lazarus, R. and Folkman, S. (1984) *Stress Appraisal and Coping*. New York: Springer.

Marriner, A. (1979) Assertive behaviour for nursing leaders. In *Nursing Leadership*, **2**(4), 14–20.

Nichols, K. and Jenkinson, J. (1991) *Leading a Support Group*. London: Chapman and Hall.

Nichols, K., Springford, V. and Searle, J. (1981) An investigation of distress and discontent in various types of nursing. In *Journal of Advanced Nursing*, **6**, 311–318.

Oskins, S. (1979) Identification of situational stressors and coping methods by intensive care nurses. In *Heart and Lung*, **8**(5), 953–960.

Pearlin, L. and Schooler, C. (1978) The structure of coping. In *J. Health Soc. Behav.*, **19**(2), 32–40.

Schmalenberg, C. and Kramer, M. (1979) Bicultural training: a cost effective programme. In *Journal of Nursing Administration*, December, 10–16.

Selye, H. (1956) *The Stress of Life*. New York: McGraw-Hill.

Topf, M. (1989) Personality hardiness, occupational stress and burnout in critical care nurses. In *Research in Nursing and Health*, **12**, 179–186.

Chapter 9

Abbey, J. (1980) FANCAP: What is it? In Riehl, J. P. and Roy, C. (eds), *Conceptual Models for Nursing Practice*, 2nd edn, 1984. Norwalk, Connecticut: Appleton & Lange.

Aggleton, P. and Chalmers, H. (1989) Working with the Riehl Model of Nursing. In Riehl-Sisca, J. P., *Conceptual Models for Nursing Practice*, 3rd edn, 1989. Norwalk, Connecticut: Appleton & Lange.

Arumugam, U. (1985) Helping Harry to relate. In *Nursing Times*, 22 June, pp 43–45.

Arumugam, U. (1989) The Riehl model in practice with families and with staff. In Riehl-Sisca, J. P. (ed), *Conceptual Models for Nursing Practice*, 3rd edn, 1989. Norwalk, Connecticut: Appleton & Lange.

Campbell, A. (1984) *Moderated Love – a Philosophy of Professional Caring*. London: SPCK.

Ersser, S. (1991) *Primary Nursing in Perspective*. London: Scutari.

HMSO (1991) *The Patient's Charter*, London: Her Majesty's Stationery Office.

Jolley, M. (1992) *Contemporary Thinking in Nursing Care: the Challenge of Change*. London: Edward Arnold.

Riehl-Sisca, J. P. (ed.) (1989) *Conceptual Models for Nursing Practice*, 3rd edn. Norwalk, Connecticut: Appleton & Lange.

Stevens, B. J. (1984) *Nursing Theory, Analysis, Application, Evaluation*, 2nd edn. Norwalk, Connecticut: Appleton & Lange.

UKCC (1986) *Project 2000: a New Preparation for Practice*. London: United Kingdom Central Council for Nursing, Midwifery and Health Visiting.

Wright, S. (1990) *My Patient, My Nurse*. London: Scutari.